TURNING THE PAGE

This is an exciting period for the book, a time of innovation, experimentation, and change. It is also a time of considerable fear within the book industry as it adjusts to changes in how books are created and consumed. The movement to digital has been taking place for some time, but with consumer books experiencing the transition, the effects of digitization can be clearly seen by everybody.

In *Turning the Page* Angus Phillips analyses the fundamental drivers of the book publishing industry – authorship, readership, and copyright – and examines the effects of digital and other developments on the book itself.

Drawing on theory and research across a range of subjects, from business and sociology to neuroscience and psychology, and from interviews with industry professionals, Phillips investigates how the fundamentals of the book industry are changing in a world of ebooks, self-publishing, and emerging business models. Useful comparisons are also made with other media industries which have undergone rapid change, such as music and newspapers.

This book is an ideal companion for anyone wishing to understand the transition of the book, writing, and publishing in recent years and will be particularly relevant to students studying publishing, media, and communications.

Angus Phillips is Director of the Oxford International Centre for Publishing Studies at Oxford Brookes University. He is the author of *Inside Book Publishing* (with Giles Clark), editor of *The Future of the Book in the Digital Age* (with Bill Cope), and Editor-in-Chief of the premier publishing journal *Logos*.

'It is one of the on-going ironies of the book business that while each year it surpasses the amount of content produced in previous years, its output reflects so little on itself. Angus Phillips' new book redresses the balance, and will be enjoyed by a wide range of people – from publishers (actual and potential) to keen readers. His broad frame of reference is particularly welcome; accessing research from a wide variety of disciplines and mixing this with both reflection on his own experiences and those of a wide range of industry professionals and other stakeholders. Consistently illuminating, enlightening and fascinating, this important book offers the tempting prospect of time well spent.'

Alison Baverstock, *Course Leader, MA Publishing, Kingston University*

'*Turning the Page* is essential reading for anyone interested in how books are changing. Covering all the key topics in a clear and comprehensive fashion, Phillips raises vital questions about authorship, copyright and the very form of the book itself. With a wide and judicious set of examples, there is no better place to learn about the emerging ecosystem of the digital book.'

Michael Bhaskar, *Digital Publishing Director, Profile Books and author of* The Content Machine

'Angus Phillips has produced a concise, lively, engaged study of key themes affecting the present and future of the book, offering in erudite yet accessible form insights into reading, publishing and content creation in a digital age. A must for those thinking through how the publishing industry might respond to the challenges of the digital world.'

David Finkelstein, *Dean, School of Humanities, University of Dundee*

'As a key industry expert, Phillips can be trusted to present us with a level-headed assessment of the radical transformations the book trade is currently experiencing.'

Adriaan van der Weel, *Bohn Professor of Book Studies, University of Leiden*

TURNING THE PAGE

The evolution of the book

Angus Phillips

LONDON AND NEW YORK

First published 2014
by Routledge
2 Park Square, Milton Park, Abingdon, Oxon OX14 4RN

and by Routledge
711 Third Avenue, New York, NY 10017

Routledge is an imprint of the Taylor & Francis Group, an informa business

© 2014 Angus Phillips

The right of Angus Phillips to be identified as author of this work has been asserted in accordance with sections 77 and 78 of the Copyright, Designs and Patents Act 1988.

All rights reserved. No part of this book may be reprinted or reproduced or utilised in any form or by any electronic, mechanical, or other means, now known or hereafter invented, including photocopying and recording, or in any information storage or retrieval system, without permission in writing from the publishers.

Trademark notice: Product or corporate names may be trademarks or registered trademarks, and are used only for identification and explanation without intent to infringe.

British Library Cataloguing in Publication Data
A catalogue record for this book is available from the British Library

Library of Congress Cataloging in Publication Data
Phillips, Angus, 1961–
Turning the page : the evolution of the book / Angus Phillips.
pages cm
Includes bibliographical references and index.
1. Electronic publishing. 2. Electronic books. 3. Authorship. 4. Books and reading. 5. Copyright. 6. Book industries and trade--Technological innovations. I. Title.
Z286.E43P53 2014
070.5--dc23
2013030112

ISBN: 978-0-415-62564-7 (hbk)
ISBN: 978-0-415-62565-4 (pbk)
ISBN: 978-0-203-10339-5 (ebk)

Typeset in Bembo
by Taylor & Francis Books

For Ann, Matthew, Charlotte, and Jamie

CONTENTS

List of illustrations		viii
Preface		ix
Introduction		xi
1	The democratization of authorship	1
2	Slow books	24
3	Condemned to be free? Content in a digital world	51
4	Digital capital	73
5	The global book	99
6	Diversity and convergence	116
Bibliography		129
Index		136

ILLUSTRATIONS

Figures

0.1 Key drivers	xii
2.1 Literacy rates in Brazil	33
4.1 Knowledge-based strategy	92
4.2 Linear model	93
4.3 Network model with feedback	93
4.4 Digital capital	94
5.1 Core–periphery model	108

Tables

2.1 Mean time spent per day on reading and watching TV	29
2.2 Demographics for reading books in the UK	31
4.1 Top ten books in social media, November 2012	83
5.1 Top ten languages from which translations have been made since 1979	107
5.2 Target languages for translations since 1979	107

PREFACE

This book takes its inspiration from the many conversations I have had with industry professionals and fellow academics from around the world. It is an exciting and challenging time for the publishing industry and this work is an opportunity to take a step back and look at the fundamentals of the industry before turning to examine the book itself.

I also take inspiration from my own love of the book. There is a rule in my household that as one book arrives, another must leave to make room, but I have broken this on many an occasion, whether through double shelving or the piles of books which find themselves appearing on free surfaces. I am happy now reading on an electronic device and it is amazing to be able to download an ebook and start reading within seconds, but I still read and collect print books.

A further inspiration has been the children's author Arthur Ransome. My family and I have spent a number of family holidays in the Lake District in the north-west of England, either out on the lakes or climbing the fells. Staying on the shores of Coniston, we have canoed out with our packed lunch to Peel Island, which bears considerable resemblance to Wild Cat Island in his *Swallows and Amazons* and where Ransome himself would have picnicked. We have also followed my daughter as she has attempted to find the definitive place to match the hidden valley of Swallowdale, which gives its name to the second book in the series. I can remember my first reading of *Swallows and Amazons* as a child, and the world of adventure opened up by the book, and it has given me great pleasure to see that this world continues to appeal to my children. When I bought a volume of Ransome's letters, I discovered that he went to Russia in 1914 and wrote a guide to St Petersburg in only four weeks, amounting to 60,000 words. This book is slightly over that length and if I have faltered on the way, there was always the knowledge that anything is possible.

There are a number of people who gave up their time to be interviewed and to whom I owe a debt of gratitude: Michael Bhaskar, Carlo Carrenho, Fu Chenzhou,

Lindsey Davis, Jackie Huang, Ou Hong, Miha Kovač, Yang Li, Jo Lusby, Simon Meek, Craig Mod, Natalie Phillips, Cheng Sanguo, Mike Shatzkin, Rüdiger Wischenbart, Fangzhou Yang, and Barbara J. Zitwer. I am also grateful for the receipt of a research scholarship from Santander Universities.

To colleagues at Ljubljana University, Moscow State University of Printing Arts of Ivan Fyodorov, and Peking University, I offer my thanks for their hospitality and kindness; and to all my colleagues at the Oxford International Centre for Publishing Studies at Oxford Brookes University for their continuing support and good humour. At Routledge a number of people helped this book along its way: Aileen Storry, Sheni Kruger, Sarah Douglas, and the copy-editor, Kate Reeves.

For their invaluable comments on earlier drafts of the text, I would like to thank Michael Bhaskar, Giles Clark, Miha Kovač, and Charlotte Phillips.

INTRODUCTION

This is an exciting period for the book, a time of innovation, experimentation, and change. It is also a time of considerable fear within the book industry as it adjusts to changes in how books are created and consumed. The movement to digital has been taking place for some time, but with consumer books experiencing the transition, the effects of digitization can be clearly seen by everybody.

This book does not attempt to cover the form and functions of the publishing industry. I do that elsewhere.[1] Instead the aim is to analyse the fundamental drivers of the book publishing industry, and to examine the effects of digital and other developments on the book itself. The three drivers I identify are authorship, readership, and copyright, on which the world of book publishing depends. Books need authors and readers, and the business of books relies on a regime in which intellectual property can be exploited and protected.

The perspective I am taking is from the field of publishing studies, and given its interdisciplinary nature, I have drawn on theory and research from a range of subjects from business and sociology to neuroscience and psychology. Since other media have experienced digital transformations ahead of the book, I have investigated what has been happening in the areas of music and newspapers. In addition to drawing on my own observations of the book industry worldwide, I have conducted a series of interviews with industry professionals, from authors to digital publishers. Although my viewpoint is of the book internationally, inevitably there is a bias towards my own direct experience of the UK market for books.

Digital tide

The volume's focus is on trade – or consumer – publishing, the area in which the coming of digital is being felt most at the moment. In particular, there has been a marked movement towards ebooks in adult fiction. If you take the areas of journals

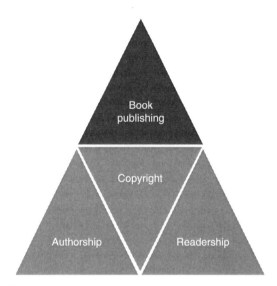

FIGURE 0.1 Key drivers

or professional publishing, the transition to digital has largely been made, and the area of educational publishing is much affected by government policy. The field of digital publishing is fast moving and there would be little point for this book to attempt analysis of the latest publishing start-up or the monthly statistics around ebook sales. In the US market, the most developed for ebooks, whilst the *pace* of growth appeared by 2013 to be slowing, ebooks had made deep inroads into parts of the market, most prominently fiction.

I have likened the impact of digital on the world of publishing to the tide coming in, up a beach.[2] There are islands of sand which remain unaffected, but gradually the water washes into every area. There are parts of the world where print remains the dominant medium, but as the internet and mobile technology spread ever further, the water continues to rise. It may be construction workers reading on mobile phones in China, children learning on tablet computers in Turkey, or commuters using their dedicated ereaders on the Metro in Russia.

The whole debate over print vs. digital is over. Reading on screen is here and the arrival of mobile devices and ereaders means it is happening all around us – on the train, at the bus stop, and on the beach. The transition to digital also means that we can move on from the discussion of the death of the book – the shape of the argument was that the book would disappear in the face of an onslaught from a range of visual media competing for our attention.[3] The book is evolving in the digital environment, experimentation is taking place yet, perhaps to the surprise of some, it is still with us. We can now start to look at how the book is developing and how it might change in the future.

If the book was becoming an irrelevance, it is also surprising how it has attracted the attention of the large technology players, from Google, attracted by its quality content, to Apple, whose co-founder originally declared the book of no interest whatsoever. One of the biggest players on the internet, Amazon, started its business in the area of books and went on to develop an ereader which cracked open the market for reading on screen for pleasure rather than simply for work. The low marginal cost of an ebook should in theory make publishing more profitable, especially if the market can be expanded, as income rises above the fixed costs. However, lower entry costs mean that traditional publishing houses face competition from self-publishing by authors, literary agents publishing their authors' backlists, publishing start-ups, and booksellers such as Amazon with their own publishing operations. There is disruption to the economy of the book from the content, often user-generated, available online. All this is against a backdrop of falling print sales in some markets. Further, as the act of copying loses value, the expectation of users is that books should be inexpensive or even free.

We have a whole new range of terminology around the book, brought about by digital developments. For the simple conversion of a printed text, we can talk about the *vanilla* ebook, and we have both *enhanced* ebooks (with the addition of audio and video) and *born digital* books – new products developed specifically for devices such as the iPad. For marketing reasons publishers may still call these products books, but traditional routes of production are being left behind. The printed book has had to step gracefully aside and allow itself to be called the pbook.

Reading is taking place across a host of devices from the PC to mobile phones and dedicated readers such as the Kindle or Nook. It is possible to carry on reading a book from the same place in the text, having switched from your ereader to your phone. Meanwhile print is not going away, and offers the advantages of a tactile experience, ready ownership, an object of pride, and a store of memories.

For writers there are more avenues than ever before through which to make their work available, with the opportunity to experiment openly and receive feedback from readers. Anyone can now publish a book in print, online, or as an ebook, and sell their work direct. The world of authorship is now more democratic, but with an oversupply of titles the chances of bestsellerdom are slim.

The big themes

Some large themes dominate the discussion of the evolution of the book, and how these play out form the backdrop to the analysis. They impact in significant ways on the key drivers of authorship, readership, and copyright examined in the first three chapters.

First, *disintermediation*, with the arrival of digital production and distribution enabling the bypassing of traditional players in the value chain of publishing and the arrival of new ones. Do authors need publishers? Do readers need physical bookshops? Author can talk direct to reader, publisher direct to consumer, technology company direct to user. The old patterns of content creation and distribution are being worn away, and much experimentation is taking place. J. K. Rowling is selling her ebooks direct to her readers, Amazon has its own publishing operation, and readers are investing directly in the production of new titles.

xiv Introduction

Second, *globalization* – with the arrival of ebooks, readers the other side of the world do not have to wait for a book to be printed and distributed, or translated. They can download the book on first publication and have immediate access. This is a tremendous opportunity for books and knowledge to spread in new ways, across new networks. Countries without a developed infrastructure for the distribution of physical books can access content directly. But does the arrival of ebooks signal an even greater dominance for books published in the English language?

Third, *convergence*, which takes many forms. These include the presence of many types of media on the same mobile device, where the book has to compete directly with games, newspapers, the web, and social media. This brings opportunities but also considerable risk for the book's future. There is also convergence of people's tastes around the latest cross-media franchise, of which books remain a key part; and convergence in the minds of users, who will be less able to differentiate categories of media, and will be making connections between content in new ways.

Last, *discoverability* – how on earth will readers come to find books? Authors can self-publish their work, a publisher can put a book on Amazon, a book app can be posted on iTunes – but how does anybody know it is there? If the high street bookshop or public library is to disappear, serendipitous discoveries while browsing new and backlist titles will be a thing of the past, to be replaced by what? This has yet to be determined – will it be social media which provides the answer, or highly targeted advertising based on our reading habits?

The book itself

What will happen to the book itself? The advocates of containerization maintain that the book is simply an outmoded vessel for content. It should be broken up, just as has happened to the music album, and in doing so this will bring down the publishing houses which want to retain control. The book is a container of content, ripe for being distributed and sold as separate chapters or in whatever form makes sense. This will facilitate a standardized, low price – or even freely available content – whilst the job of assembly can switch to new curators of content. Users themselves can create personalized selections, collections, and mixed-media works. Books no longer need be square, rectangular, with boundaries; they can be any format or length, free of the restrictions imposed by print. Already we can see a return to shorter forms of writing, such as short stories and novellas, and serialized fiction which responds almost in real time to the market.

I have taken as a subtitle 'The evolution of the book' because what I can see is not a dramatic tearing-up of the old forms. The most successful form of the book in the digital world has so far been the vanilla ebook – the economic model works, just about, and this is because it replicates, now with some advantages, how the printed book operates. You can create an all-singing, all-dancing book, but most such projects have lost money against high production costs. They have also brought the book into direct competition with products from gaming and other media companies, which have big pockets and limited product lines.

The book can become larger or smaller, faster to market, expand its horizons to encompass multimedia, or content itself with linear text which stimulates thought and imagination. There is no one set path, and there are different branches to be explored as the book evolves.

Notes

1 Giles Clark and Angus Phillips, *Inside Book Publishing*, 5th edition, Routledge, 2014.
2 Angus Phillips, 'The Digital Tide in Europe', paper given at the World Book Summit, Ljubljana, Slovenia, 31 March 2011.
3 See, for example, Angus Phillips, 'Does the Book have a Future?', in Simon Eliot and Jonathan Rose, *A Companion to the History of the Book*, Blackwell, 2007.

1

THE DEMOCRATIZATION OF AUTHORSHIP

Are you serious about this? Then get an accountant.

Hilary Mantel's first rule for writers[1]

Self-evidently, the book would not exist without authors. The food chain of publishing relies on authors, most of whom are not writing in the expectation of making a living. Some write to supplement their income from the day job, academic authors wish to advance their careers, and many just feel the urge to put pen to paper (or most likely type on screen). It is part of who they are – they know they want to write.

With annual income from authorship running at a low level, on average around £11,000 in the UK, the large majority of writers do not earn enough to support themselves.[2] They are most likely to have other careers alongside. The paradox is that writing and getting published in book form remain desirable, whilst there are many new avenues for writers to be heard. If you want to write, you can post a daily blog and reach thousands of readers in an immediate way. Yet, when the British prime minister Tony Blair wanted to write the story of his premiership, it was not a blog he produced; he wanted to put his version of events on record – and a book remains the best way of doing that.

The coming of digital enables innovation and experimentation by authors, from self-publishing to new forms of writing, and so far these developments can be seen most clearly in author-led publishing and in particular in the area of genre fiction.

Making it as an author

Getting taken on by a publisher remains difficult, which of course adds to its desirability. For a first-time novelist, for example, the chances of being noticed and picked up by a mainstream publishing house remain low. Publishers no longer

2 The democratization of authorship

maintain a slush pile of manuscripts to pick through – most trade houses will not accept unsolicited submissions. In the area of fiction they expect to work through literary agents, and the trend has been to shift the sifting of talent in that direction. Agents in turn may prefer to work on personal recommendation from contacts or existing clients. There will always be the story of a new author being picked up from the mail box, and this does still happen, but it is a rare event. However they are discovered, working in a new author's favour is that publishers are always on the look-out for a new star around which a story can be built to promote them. To the detriment of 'mid-list' authors still developing their career, who may find themselves dropped by publishers and agents, there is pressure to find the next new talent.

Agents are largely a phenomenon of the Anglo-US publishing system, and in the UK they began to appear at the end of the nineteenth century. This coincided with a boom in print publishing, the strengthening of the copyright regime internationally, and sufficient economic and other rewards for writers.[3] In the terms of the French sociologist Pierre Bourdieu, writers acquired considerable cultural capital and notable authors were feted and celebrated. Employing an agent could benefit authors financially through better terms from publishers, and also increase their status by emphasizing their role as a professional. After their initial hostility towards agents, publishers over time came to appreciate the advantages of an intermediary who could select and nurture talent. In the present multi-channel environment, trade authors have come to rely heavily on their agents. Selling rights to a range of other media can be highly important, from film and TV to computer games, in addition to selling translation rights and an assortment of electronic rights.

Agents are a rarity in Continental Europe, perhaps because there is generally less money in the system by comparison to the globalized markets of English language publishing. In France, for example, the first whispers of the entry of literary agents in the 1990s were greeted with some horror by French publishers, who believed that their presence would alter or destroy what had 'previously been a sacrosanct relation between artist and editor'.[4] Further, there was the belief that the precarious nature of French literature publishing would be destabilized. Examination of practices around the payment of royalties showed that a first-time novelist might only receive any royalty at all once a certain sales threshold was reached.

A stir was caused a decade later when the American author Jonathan Littell decided to use an agent to sell the rights in his novel *Les Bienveillantes* (2006) to a French publisher whilst retaining the rights in other languages. He first wrote the book in French and it was later published in English as *The Kindly Ones* (2009). The significance of his step in acting through an agent was amplified by the rave reception given to the book: it won both the Prix Goncourt and the Prix du Roman de l'Académie française. Interviewed in *Le Monde des livres*, Littell said:

> In the Anglo-Saxon world if you want to publish a book, you look for an agent first. So I never thought to do anything else. This French notion of

sending your manuscript direct to a publishing house is foreign to me. I do understand that it worries some people in France, where a delicate balancing act ensures that certain books are published which would never be elsewhere. That system has a cost. In France, barely any authors make a living; the entire chain profits from the book, except the writer.[5]

A 2007 survey of UK and German authors found that authors operate in an environment of 'winner takes all'. In the UK the top 10 per cent of professional authors (defined as those who allocate more than 50 per cent of their time to writing) earned 60 per cent of total income, whilst in Germany the top 10 per cent earned 41 per cent. By contrast the bottom 50 per cent in the UK earned 8 per cent of total income; in Germany the bottom 50 per cent earned 12 per cent of total income. The market was more highly skewed in the UK, where 7.2 per cent of authors earned £100,000 or more from writing, whilst in the sample of German authors, just 1.7 per cent of writers earned £100,000 or more.[6] This may reflect the wider reach of the English language throughout the world, or a higher rate of translation from English into other languages. The inescapable conclusion of the research was that most authors could not make a living without having another source of income. A 2012 survey of advance payments to authors in the UK found that 19 per cent of authors received no payment; 40 per cent up to £5,000; a further 19 per cent up to £15,000; and 22 per cent received an advance of over £15,000.[7]

Other routes to finding a publisher include enrolling on a creative writing course. The boom in these courses in recent years again reflects the popularity of writing: taking the USA as an example, there are over 800 progammes in existence. The courses provide employment for published writers (famously Martin Amis was a professor at Manchester University in the UK), and students benefit from advice from their tutor and fellow students. Most courses are based around the writing workshop, in which students read out samples of their work to fellow students. The literature academic Louis Menand describes the workshop as a 'process, an unscripted performance space, a regime for forcing people to do two things that are fundamentally contrary to human nature: actually write stuff (as opposed to planning to write stuff very, very soon), and then sit there whilst strangers tear it apart'.[8] Opinions differ as to the value of creative writing courses – is it the case that writers can be taught? – but there is no doubting the success of the better programmes, which attract talent and in turn both agents and publishers, keen to spot the latest hot property.

The novelist Will Self is a sceptic when it comes to creative writing programmes:

> Perhaps you can take a mediocre novelist and make them into a slightly better one, but a course can't make someone into a good writer. Ian McEwan and Kazuo Ishiguro both did the UEA [University of East Anglia] MA, but they were both innately good anyway. Some people swear by

4 The democratization of authorship

creative writing courses. I say, go and get a job, a fairly menial one instead. Otherwise what are you going to write about? Writing is about expressing something new and exploring the form in new ways. So unless you want to churn out thrillers or misery memoirs, you can't work from a pattern book.[9]

A whole industry to help authors has developed, from writing academies run by mainstream publishers to editorial services which will rewrite proposals or complete manuscripts. Such operations have been criticized for taking advantage of authors and acting as routes for monetizing the slush pile. There is a further option available to the budding author, that of self-publishing, which can lead to being taken on by a conventional publishing house, having served as a means of getting noticed and attracting a following. For many authors, self-publishing may simply provide the satisfaction of finding an audience, with a chance of making some money. Forms of self-publishing range from publication in ebook form to posting work on a community website.

Self-publishing

Once dismissed as vanity publication, self-publishing is now an established path with an ever-growing degree of respectability. If successful, there is the possibility of being signed up by a publisher, who has seen the author's market potential. Some of the large publishing houses have their own self-publishing operations; for example, Penguin bought the self-publishing platform Author Solutions in 2012. Print publication is possible, through a variety of routes, and the use of digital printing can keep print runs low and still affordable. A work can be posted on the internet as a pdf file and downloaded by readers to be read on screen or printed out. Publication of an ebook – to be read on dedicated devices or a tablet computer – offers a quick and direct route to market. For example, signing up with Amazon offers an author a direct share of the proceeds from sales without the normal share taken by a publisher. The share of income can be up to 70 per cent on low-priced titles. For established authors, with a strong presence in the market, the sale of ebooks offers the opportunity to increase their royalty rates too. If they retain the electronic rights, there are companies willing to offer them high rates (up from an industry norm of 25 per cent to 50 or 60 per cent) for sales on an exclusive basis through Amazon.

So why would an author not go ahead and publish their own book? The mechanisms are there and the royalty rates are much higher than if they worked through a publisher. The echoes of the vanity press have largely disappeared, and you can find self-published authors on *The New York Times* bestseller list. For some this approach has definitely worked – take the thriller writer John Locke, the first self-published author to sell 1m Kindle ebooks. He knew there was little point in operating as a print publisher of his own books:

I learned early in the game I couldn't compete with the big boys and girls in their arena of hardcover and paperback books. The famous authors have huge corporations backing them, newspaper ads and reviews promoting them, and bookstores displaying them. As a self-published author, I'm boxed out of these marketing opportunities. Worse, I can't afford to offer my print books as cheaply as they can![10]

But with the advent of a consumer market for ebooks, he found he could compete, and price his books for as little as 99 cents. In fact the low price worked to his advantage, because the risk to the reader is minimized when they are paying out less than a dollar. He also writes across different genres, including crime and westerns, under the same name, whereas established publishing practice is that separate brands should be established so as not to risk disappointing readers.

The strategy of digital first also worked well for the US writer Hugh Howie, who published his short story *Wool* as an ebook in July 2011. Three months later he noticed sales starting to increase rapidly, so he started on a second part and attracted a highly engaged audience eager for more. He said:

I liken it to the difference between recording an album in a studio and playing live. When you play live it's you and an audience and you get energy from the applause. Every day I was getting emails, Facebook posts and tweets. It was energising knowing I was writing for an audience. I've hidden my phone number in one of the books and people find it and call me randomly. It's awkward when it happens but I like that blatant transparency about everything. This ride's not going to last forever and why not just enjoy it?[11]

The book expanded into a five-part novel and he resisted selling digital rights to a US publisher, since sales were going well without such a deal, although he did sell print only rights to Simon & Schuster.

The market for self-published works is still developing, but early evidence again suggests characteristics of 'winner takes all' with rewards concentrated in favour of a small percentage of authors. Of those self-published authors surveyed in a study published in 2012, half earned less than $500 from their books in 2011. The top earning 10 per cent of authors earned 75 per cent of the total royalties reported by the respondents. These authors tended to have published more titles, but also their books generated 11 times more royalty revenue.[12] The industry thinker Mike Shatzkin says there is a need for self-published authors to keep their output high: 'All of the best self-published writers – or the most successful ones – say that one of the key things is to be prolific. Keep feeding the beast, because what happens is you get fans, and they will keep buying the stuff you make available. But it you stop, they will forget about you.'[13] Lindsey Davis, former chair of the Society of Authors in the UK, and author of the Falco series of crime novels, sees the work involved in self-publishing and the limited chances of success:

6 The democratization of authorship

> To self-publish properly you have to put in a lot of time, which means you don't have that time for writing. You have to – to do it properly – invest money. For every one or two big names that you get who actually make a huge success of it ... there are thousands and thousands who only sell a few hundred books.[14]

Highly successful as a self-published writer, Amanda Hocking sold over 1m ebooks as an author of young adult fiction. She became even better known in 2011 as a result of her decision to sign up with the mainstream publisher, St Martin's Press. Having done all the hard work of making a name for herself, why then did she change course and allow herself to be wooed by a number of large publishers? The auction resulted in her winning a four-book deal for her Watersong series worth $2m. Partly she was keen to see her books available in bricks-and-mortar stores, and partly she wanted to concentrate on writing. On her blog, in response to the shocked response of some of her fans, she wrote of the stress involved in self-publishing, including trying to sort out decent editing of her work – 'tighten up sentences, watching repeated phrases, helping with flow, etc.' In a further post she said: 'I'm a writer. I want to be a writer. I do not want to spend 40 hours a week handling emails, formatting covers, finding editors, etc. Right now, being me is a full time corporation ... I am spending so much time on things that are not writing.'[15] Her views are echoed by J. K. Rowling, who commented on her business empire: 'it's a real bore. Should I be more diplomatic? Oh, I don't care. No, there is literally nothing on the business side that I wouldn't sacrifice in a heartbeat to have an extra couple of hours' writing.'[16]

Rowling is an example of a successful author who was reluctant to allow her books to be made available in digital form, fearing the risk from piracy. But in 2011 she ventured into self-publishing and went ahead with making all the Harry Potter titles available as ebooks, exclusively on her own website Pottermore. Asked about her decision to make the site the only retailer of the ebooks, she said that 'it was quite straightforward for me ... it means we can guarantee people everywhere are getting the same experience and at the same time. I am personally lucky to have the resources to do it myself and I could do it, I think, right.'[17] In the midst of the Harry Potter phenomenon, J. K. Rowling needed neither extra income from ebooks nor any extra exposure for the boy wizard. Although her books were pirated, both in print and on the internet, this did little to dent her sales. Her vision for Pottermore is as more than just a vehicle to sell ebooks – she is developing her own community around the books in digital form. She also now feels that one way to reduce piracy is to have a legitimate route to buy the books in digital form.

Another writer with views on piracy is the Brazilian author Paulo Coelho, famous for his allegorical novel, *The Alchemist* (1988). His publisher, HarperCollins, was perhaps not surprised to discover pirated editions of his work on the internet, but they were certainly horrified when they found out that the author himself was putting up copies of his works for free. Speaking to *The New York Times*, he shared the benefits of self-piracy:

The democratization of authorship **7**

> I saw the first pirated edition of one of my books, so I said I'm going to post
> it online. There was a difficult moment in Russia; they didn't have much
> paper. I put this first copy online and I sold, in the first year, 10,000 [print]
> copies there. And in the second year it jumped to 100,000 copies. So I said,
> 'It is working.' Then I started putting other books online, knowing that if
> people read a little bit and they like it, they are going to buy the book.
> My sales were growing and growing, and one day I was at a high-tech
> conference, and I made it public.[18]

Some would see this approach as self-defeating – just as if everybody ignores a
notice not to walk on the grass – but it is true that putting content out there for
people to read is one of the best means of promotion. We can see this with the
opportunity to read sample chapters – either printed at the end of an author's
previous book, or available as an ebook download – which encourages readers to
try a new author, or whet their appetite for an author's next book.

Promotion

Coelho has certainly hit on one aspect of an author's job that has become
increasingly important: self-promotion. Whether self-published or issued by a
mainstream house, authors need to get themselves known and noticed. Charlie
Higson, author of the Young Bond series for children, says that what is often
overlooked by writers is the need to sell themselves: 'These days a writer must do a
lot of singing and dancing, effectively selling themselves to an audience. But this is
nothing new – Charles Dickens used to hold reading events to promote his
works.'[19]

Juliet Gardiner writes of a shift in emphasis from author production to author
'promotion', which since the 1990s has even entered the realm of literary fiction.
Whereas before it was possible to have a romantic view of the author as remote
from the commercial world of the mass market, now all authors have to carry out a
performative role:

> the promotable fiction author who spends, say, a year writing a novel, will
> now spend considerably more than a year promoting it in a round of press,
> radio, and television interviews, bookshop readings, and other events on
> publication – a circuit that is replicated whenever and wherever across the
> globe the book is subsequently published.[20]

But what of those authors who wish to remain in their garret, allowing their
work to speak for itself? There are some, such as the recluse J. D. Salinger, who
will do just fine. Shortly after the publication of *The Catcher in the Rye* in 1951, he
retreated from the world and only rarely offered himself up to be interviewed. The
novelist John Updike was seldom called on to perform in the early years of his
writing career:

8 The democratization of authorship

> In my first 15 or 20 years of authorship, I was almost never asked to give a speech or an interview. The written work was supposed to speak for itself, and to sell itself, sometimes even without the author's photograph on the back flap. As the author is gradually retired from his old responsibilities of vicarious confrontation and provocation, he has grown in importance as a kind of walking, talking advertisement for the book – a much more pleasant and flattering duty, it may be, than composing the book in solitude.[21]

In the banquet speech given when he was awarded the Nobel Prize for Literature in 1954, Ernest Hemingway said that: 'Writing, at its best, is a lonely life. ... [The author] grows in public stature as he sheds his loneliness and often his work deteriorates. For he does his work alone and if he is a good enough writer he must face eternity, or the lack of it, each day.'[22]

There are opportunities for authors to build a fan base who will remain expectant for the author's next book. Some authors of literary fiction, like Donna Tartt, will not rush to provide the next book. Her bestseller *The Secret History* was published in 1992, and it was ten years later that *The Little Friend* came out. But John Grisham said he received a good piece of advice early in his career – 'the big boys come out every year' – and he locked himself away to finish *The Pelican Brief* (he was at that time half way through writing the book), taking only 60 days.[23] A writer with an even more prolific output is James Patterson, who in September 2009 signed a contract to write 17 books by the end of 2012. How was he able to make such a commitment? He has a team of co-authors, working with him on crime novels as well as science fiction, romance and YA (young adult) novels, and is another author happy to defy publishing convention by writing across genres under the same name. He is sold under the slogan, 'James Patterson – The pages turn themselves'.[24]

Even if authors disavow media opportunities and a series of appearances at literary festivals, book slams, and bookshop signings, they will still be encouraged to make use of social media such as Facebook and Twitter. Most big-name authors have their own websites, blogs, and Twitter feeds – it is just expected. In 2011 a new author joined the fray on Twitter, as commented on by Jon Henley in the *Guardian*:

> You are, by any standards, a modern-day literary colossus. Your novels are fat, fantastical, fatwa-inducing and famously difficult to finish. You've won the Whitbread (twice), the Booker and the Booker of Bookers; are photographed, frequently, in the company of wildly beautiful women much younger (and taller) than yourself; have been elevated to a knighthood by Her Majesty the Queen. What kingdoms remain for you to conquer, what realms still defy your dominion? ... Well, Twitter, for one.[25]

Salman Rushdie, bestselling author of novels such as *Midnight's Children* (1981), appeared on Twitter in 2011. When, in January 2012, he was advised that his appearance at the Jaipur Literary Festival in India might cause security issues, he cancelled his appearance there. What made the news was not just his cancellation but also his Twitter silence on the issue.

One of the perils of social media is the direct communication with your readers. In 2012 the UK author of the mountain cliffhanger *Touching the Void*, Joe Simpson, found himself on the end of abuse from students who were studying his book for a school (GCSE) examination. Among the tweets he received were:

> hi joe. i had an exam about your book. I failed because of you. you owe to me!
> even my english teacher couldn't get past the first 5 chapters
> YOUR BOOK IS THE REASON MY ENTIRE YEAR WILL FAIL OUR ENGLISH EXAM!!LEARN TO WRITE ILLITERATE FOOL!
> Are you all ready and set for your hate on your book because of the exams?[26]

The author developed a robust line of responses, including:

> … a lovely day of children writhing in their hellish hormonal middens …
> good night vile innocents may you all seethe in bilious acid pus …
> Bye bye brainless boy!
> Ok bored of this now so I'll either stop twitter or block all school kids – shame on the good ones – but the loathesome scroats can sod off!

In the end the author concluded: 'At one point I thought it was a great honour to have your book slated for the GCSE and now I'm beginning to think it's a pain in the arse, frankly.'[27]

Authoring on the web

The web provides a range of opportunities for authors wishing to make their work public. A work can be posted on the author's own website, and that may be enough. Writers can experiment with new genres or categories, such as flash fiction, stories of up to a thousand words. There are community sites – for example Wattpad, styled as the YouTube for electronic stories – which offer easy posting of your writing, whether in full or serial form. In 2012, Wattpad attracted a new member every two-and-a-half seconds and 10m unique visitors each month. A high percentage of users are reading the stories, and are not just writers, and it attracts genres such as romance, paranormal, and fan fiction.[28] The authonomy site (run by HarperCollins) has thousands of books posted which can be read online for free. Readers rate the works and a chart system is in operation. New authors are published having been discovered on the site, and HarperCollins has also issued ebooks of some of the titles.

Devotees of particular authors can contribute to fan fiction sites, posting chapters or fuller works in a certain style or genre. Browsing of the site fanfiction.net in

10 The democratization of authorship

2012 revealed fans of Roald Dahl, Donna Tartt, and John Boyne, author of *The Boy in the Striped Pyjamas*. The novel *Wives and Daughters* by Elizabeth Gaskell – she died (in 1865) before completing the book – offered the opportunity for readers to create their own ending. Amongst the most popular authors are Jane Austen and Tolkien, but they all trailed way behind J. K. Rowling – who had attracted over half a million contributions. In 2013 Amazon came up with a new model to monetize fan fiction, Kindle Worlds, which distributed income from ebooks both to the self-published author and the original rights holder.[29]

Fan fiction has set loose the imagination of readers in many different directions – indeed, it was J. K. Rowling herself who announced that Albus Dumbledore was gay. Genres include slash, where characters are paired off with each other in likely or unlikely relationships. An early example of this is from fans of Star Trek, who have explored the possibilities of a relationship between Captain Kirk and Mr Spock. Other genres include mpreg (the man gets pregnant) and curtainfic (where the pairing become all domestic and shop for curtains).[30]

To many readers, the idea of fan fiction might appear merely derivative and uninteresting, as Anik LaChev has observed about her passion: 'Working on fan fiction was about as prestigious as working on commercial romance novels and always went with the assumption that I clearly had no life (and certainly no love life) and thus had to make one up beneath the (book) covers of virtual bodice rippers.'[31] Yet many enthusiasts love the chance to write, share, and become part of a community. Fan fiction has come to develop its own forms, such as the drabble, which is a brief story of precisely 100 words. Also it has developed norms around writing challenges with defined limits and time-scales. Creativity is seen as more important than originality, and it may derive from interactions online. Writing about participatory culture, Henry Jenkins writes of fans:

> Unimpressed by institutional authority and expertise, the fans assert their own right to form interpretations, to offer valuations, and to construct cultural canons. Undaunted by traditional conceptions of literary and intellectual property, fans raid mass culture, claiming its materials for their own use, reworking them as the basis for their own cultural creations and social interactions. Fans seemingly blur the boundaries between fact and fiction, speaking of characters as if they had an existence apart from their textual manifestations, entering into the realm of the fiction as if it were a tangible place they can inhabit and explore.[32]

The mention of intellectual property is interesting and, as observed above, J. K. Rowling has sold enough books not to worry unduly about missing sales due to pirated editions in the Far East. By and large she has remained extremely tolerant of the range of fan fiction out there on the web, as indeed are most successful authors, who see derivative works as both a compliment and a way of spreading the word about their writing. In 2004, through her agent, Rowling gave her official reaction to the growth of Harry Potter fan fiction, saying that she was flattered by the interest in her books. Her concerns were to make sure that it remained non-commercial and that writers should ensure their stories were not obscene and were duly credited to the author (and not Rowling).

Rowling took a different view, however, when a small publisher attempted to issue a print version of a popular Harry Potter website, with the title *The Harry Potter Lexicon*. Together with Warner Brothers, which had an enormous success with the film franchise, she sued the Michigan publisher RDR Books. The case was seen as important in setting the boundaries of fan fiction and its commercial exploitation. Her reaction was reported as follows:

> Ms. Rowling harshly criticized Mr. Vander Ark and his Lexicon manuscript, calling it a compilation of phrases and facts that were taken from her book and rewritten 'without quotation marks around it,' and saying the manuscript was 'sloppy' and 'lazy.' Besides stepping on her plans to publish her own encyclopedia, she said, the Lexicon manuscript was also 'derivative' and 'riddled with errors.'
>
> 'What does it add?' she asked while on the stand. 'The idea of my readership parting with their or their parents' hard earned cash for this – I think it's a travesty.'[33]

What gave the case extra interest was that previously she had praised the website created by Steven Vander Ark – a school librarian and avid fan. Started in 2000, the site grew to 700 pages and in 2004 received a fan site award from the author – indeed she was quoted on the index page as saying 'This is such a great site … my natural home.'[34]

The possibilities of fan fiction reached new heights in commercial terms with the publication of *Fifty Shades of Grey* by E. L. James. The theory was that with ebooks, no one need know what you are reading or buying, and this was prompting increasing sales of romance and erotic fiction. But this did not go towards explaining the success of the print editions of the Fifty Shades titles as well, which showed that some readers wanted to be seen reading this kind of fiction. Jessica Weisberg wrote about the mainstream success of the books, which spawned a new genre of 'Mummy Porn':

> E. L. James, the author of the 'Fifty Shades of Grey' trilogy, is a mother and television executive in her forties. The series started as 'Twilight' fan fiction; James has said that she modelled her two main characters after Bella and Edward. Yet, even though her characters are college-aged, the books have resonated most strongly with James's contemporaries – mothers, wives, 'The View' enthusiasts – women who, if they owned riding crops, would store them in the garage between the skis and mountain bikes.[35]

Collaborative projects and mash-ups

Fan fiction offers the chance to collaborate on stories, and forms of collaborative writing have been made much easier through the use of the internet. Collaborative

12 The democratization of authorship

writing tools, such as the Vancouver-based Protagonize, enable the creation of linear stories, developed by a number of authors, as well as non-linear fiction in which a variety of authors take the story in a series of different directions.[36] Readers can navigate through this hypertext fiction, and the advent of decent ereading devices can only encourage this genre.

Non-linear fiction began in print books where the reader could make choices about the direction of a story's plot. A good example of this is the *Choose Your Own Adventure* series, written by Edward Packard and first published in the 1980s. The series was aimed at 10- to 14-year-olds, and the reader was the central character in the stories. They were faced with choices every few pages, and each option led on to one of around 40 endings. The books could be read repeatedly without rereading a page.[37] By the mid-1980s there were 30m copies in print. There were also computer adventure games based around stories, such as *The Hobbit*, through which the user progressed by typing in instructions.

Digital publication facilitates a hypertext approach to fiction. The book *Luminous Airplanes,* by Paul la Farge, was published in 2011. A young computer programmer learns that his grandfather has died, and that he has to return to Thebes, a town which is so isolated that its inhabitants have their own language, in order to clean out the house where his family lived for five generations. There he runs into Yesim, a Turkish American woman whom he loved as a child, and begins a romance in which past and present are dangerously confused. At the same time, he remembers San Francisco in the wild years of the internet boom. As well as being issued in a linear edition, both print and ebook, there is a digital edition in which the reader can take a journey around different sections of the book; there is no right order and this immersive fiction is designed so that the reader can get 'quite deep in exploring the different branches of the story'.[38] Both the conventional and the digital editions were reviewed in *The New York Times*, with the reviewer finding less of value in the online version:

> I can't recommend that you read 'Luminous Airplanes' online. Navigating the text's hyperlinks disrupts its narrative momentum, to the point that the whole thing feels like a kind of literary 52-card pickup – i.e., a lot more fun for the thrower than the throwee. The most generous take on this Web project is that it reads like a rough draft of a very good novel – which this is.[39]

The possibilities of digital texts have not yet been fully explored, perhaps because publishers remain conservative in their approach. Authors are certainly keen to experiment, and the author of the Alex Rider stories, Anthony Horowitz, is among them:

> I'd love to write a murder mystery where you could tap on a bit of dialogue you mistrusted and discover that the character was telling a lie. Where the reader had to become a detective and where the last chapter, the reveal, had

to be earned. Or how about a book with different points of view, where you could choose which of the characters became the narrator?[40]

There are also mash-ups, which take existing material and combine them or take them into a new genre. In music a track can be built up from two existing songs, for example combining Snow Patrol's 'Chasing Cars' with the Police's 'Every Breath You Take' gives you 'Every Car You Chase'.[41] A prominent example from fiction is the mixing of a zombie novel with *Pride and Prejudice* to create *Pride and Prejudice and Zombies* (2009). The book, which was a commercial hit, opens with the lines: 'It is a truth universally acknowledged that a zombie in possession of brains must be in want of more brains.' Retaining most of the original text, the mash-up adds a new level of humour by, for example, endowing the Bennet sisters with martial arts skills so that they can do battle with the undead.

Jane Austen is of course out of copyright and also needs no protection against such experimentation, given the extent of her reputation and the affection in which she is held. How, though, should the line be drawn between playful creativity and pure plagiarism? *Star Wars Uncut* is a crowdsourced homage to the original film, shot in 15-second segments by a host of amateur film-makers. Each short section could be a cartoon or live enthusiasts wearing paper helmets, drawing on the efforts of a range of fans world-wide. The film won an Emmy in the category of interactive media in 2010. Less warmly received was the book *Assassin of Secrets* by Q. R. Markham, published in 2011. Its protagonist, Jonathan Chase, was part James Bond, part Jason Bourne. Continuing in the tradition of Bond sequels written by authors other than Ian Fleming (although they were authorized by the Fleming estate), what was there not to like? Once the book was published, readers started to notice similarities in the wording to passages in other books. Indeed several had been lifted from the 1981 Bond novel by John Gardner, *Licence Renewed*. Some sentences were taken verbatim, such as the following: 'Then he saw her, behind the fountain, a small light, dim but growing to illuminate her as she stood naked but for a thin, translucent nightdress; her hair undone and falling to her waist – hair and the thin material moving and blowing as though caught in a silent zephyr.' Jeremy Duns, who had originally provided a glowing quote about the book, calling it an 'instant classic', was horrified to discover the scale of the plagiarism:

> I had hoped that this problem, awful as it was, only affected the opening of the novel, but as I looked into it more I quickly realized that the whole novel was 'written' this way – I was finding it hard to find sentences that had not been taken verbatim or near-verbatim from other sources.[42]

Was the novel an artful mash-up or perhaps a literary joke carefully designed by the author? Upon investigation, Markham turned out to be the co-owner of a Brooklyn bookstore, whose real name is Quentin Rowan. He had form in the area of plagiarism, revealed once readers started to dig around in his earlier published

14 The democratization of authorship

stories. When asked for his motivation, he said it was not a prank nor something he could satisfactorily explain. He was happy to lay out his methodology:

> I wish I was smart enough to have thought of copy-pasting. No, I sat there with the books on my kitchen table and typed the passages up word for word. I had a plot in mind, initially, and looked for passages that would work within that context. ... When I began to edit it for the publisher, that's when things really got out of hand. I was being asked to come up with whole new scenes to fit into the already stitched-up old ones. It really was like making Frankenstein's monster as people have commented. A kind of patchwork job.[43]

If he had published his work as a mash-up, he might perhaps have been lauded for his skill. However he would have been unlikely to have obtained permission to publish such an extensive set of borrowings. The publishing industry is not normally well disposed to allowing even short quotations without some kind of payment. What does this story tell us about the book? Firstly that it is perhaps less necessary to have a distinctive voice in genre fiction. Also that the web is ripe with discussion about books and this community is now a powerful force.

For those who enjoy the act of writing, the internet provides amazing room for experimentation. How much there is of value to readers remains a matter for debate. Some will enjoy treading the different pathways of a hypertext novel; others will find nothing but deep frustrations. For those longing for an eighth Harry Potter novel, fan fiction may provide some excitement; others will choose to read the original books on a regular basis.

Mobile storytelling

In an echo of the days when fiction was published in instalments – readers of *The Mystery of Edwin Drood* were left in suspense on the death of Dickens in 1870, because the author *wrote* serially too – writers of stories for mobile phones can get immediate feedback and adjust their stories as they go along. The *keitai shosetsu*, or cell-phone novel, originated in Japan and has been phenomenally successful – a free website there has over a million titles with an authorship and readership mostly of young women.[44] The phenomemon has spread to China, where for 5 yuan a month (around £0.50), you can take out a subscription which gives you a 50-book pack on your mobile phone, updated with 10 new titles each month. There are one-off sales of whole books at a low price, or of books by chapter at prices as low at 0.1 yuan each (£0.01); there is also a community of 1m authors writing for a range of literature websites. The prices may be low but the potential readership for this kind of writing is huge. There are 100m active users of Reading Base, the mobile platform run by China Mobile. For authors the rewards from the mobile phone audience may be greater than from conventional publishing. For example, whereas a print book has a limited number of pages, an online or mobile novel can carry on in the manner of a soap opera. A reader may end up paying 350 yuan (£35) for a large number of chapters – around 10 times the price of a print book. When they are paying by the chapter, they are not as sensitive to the overall price.

The mobile (and online) market in China is also subject to fewer supply-side controls compared to print books, which are required to have a book number (ISBN) issued by the state. This system enables the authorities to monitor the books published for sensitive content and also, it is argued, to maintain the profitability of the state publishing houses.[45] There are still editorial controls on mobile platforms, including removing sensitive political material (such as mention of the name of the head of state), but the number of titles can expand without limit and some genres are flourishing which would not be permitted in print. The large number of authors writing for this market suggests that the chances of finding success are slim. To make it as an author, you might have to be recommended by the editors of a literature website, or you might just find your readership by chance and shoot to the top of the site rankings. The odds are perhaps increased by the huge number of readers of online fiction overall – an estimated 200m.[46] However, only around 10,000 to 20,000 authors in China are making a reasonable living from this kind of writing. At the top end, the most popular author, Tong Jing San Chao, earned 13m yuan over a five-year period (£1.3m).[47]

Popular genres of fiction on mobile phones in China include fantasy and romance, and also local categories such as kungfu. Other genres, which have originated online, include time travel and grave robbery. The latter, adventure-horror books, have been described as the 'Indiana Jones stories of China – only with fewer fedoras and bullwhips, and more Mao caps and feng shui compasses'.[48] Authors writing what are essentially entertainments for a mass audience can gain immediate feedback on their characters and plots; new chapters may be written daily and posted both online and to the mobile audience. The temptation to keep a popular story going beyond its sell-by date is there, leading to a lack of discipline in the writing; this must be balanced against the danger of, say, killing off a popular character, which could mean that you lose your audience for that plot straight away, as well as for future titles. The Chinese writer Yang Li says that 'Chinese people like a happy ending.'[49]

A typical online work has around 3,000 to 5,000 words a chapter, and this is now easily accommodated on a mobile phone. This is helped by the fact that Chinese characters can represent whole words or meanings. Claimed as the first-ever mobile phone novel in China was *Out of Town* (2004), by Qian Fucheng. With 60 chapters, and 70 words in each chapter, this had a total of only 4,200 words. 'When I started to write this novel, I was excited, I was thinking the text message on a mobile phone should be more than just simple jokes, it should work on a higher level of literature,' the author said.

> The way of writing is totally different, because 70 characters is not enough for one sentence in the traditional novel, so I tried to discover a whole new

16 The democratization of authorship

> area of literature, and to go carefully. ... I always remind myself – less conversation and less description. As it's a novel, I need to tell the story in a good way, but I also need to save space, I cannot waste a single word, or even punctuation marks.[50]

This form of writing has not yet taken off in Western markets, but certainly there is more reading happening on mobile phones around the world. The spin-offs in print or into film and TV can be very lucrative. *Deep Love* by Yoshi, originally published in Japan as ketai in 2002, sold millions of copies as a print book and was also made into a successful film.

Blogging

In 2010 there were estimated to be around 150m blogs in the world, but many were largely inactive. Most are abandoned within only a few months as their authors find it difficult to maintain any momentum. For authors, blogs provide the opportunity to cut their writing teeth and get feedback from readers. There is money to be made out of blogs, including from advertising and sponsorship (from readers or from companies wishing to promote their products), and in order to generate these revenues, one eye has to be kept on hits and site traffic. However, it is estimated that 60 per cent of bloggers are hobbyists not wishing to seek any commercial return. These are people who blog for fun, and are happy to take the opportunity to speak their minds and record their experiences.

Blogging has attracted a whole new set of writers, with a 2006 study in the USA showing that 54 per cent of bloggers had not published anything before. The primary topic of their blogs was their life and experiences, forming a personal journal. Over half of the bloggers were under 30, and again over half used a pseudonym. The most popular reasons for keeping a blog were for the author to express themselves creatively and to share experiences. Only one-third saw their blog as a form of journalism.[51]

Blogs vary in their approach, from political commentary to more of a diary form. The style of writing is usually personal and conversational, including hyperlinks and perhaps pictures and video. Bloggers may adopt a pseudonym as a way of separating themselves from the content. This may serve to protect their private life or working interests. Some bloggers have to be careful who might read their personal information or their comments about third parties. In the UK 'Jack Night' wrote a blog about the reality of policing in modern Britain, for example writing about how he sees justice is badly served by the ability of the defendant to change his plea at the last minute when the case gets to court:

> It is here that we see the phenomenon of the 'Cracked Trial'. This is nothing to do with the popular baking soda / cocaine amalgam, it is what happens when we all turn up and the defendant throws his hand in at the very last minute. ... The way things are, you can sit on your hands as a defendant

right up to the court doors and still retain the possibility of a very chunky discount for a guilty plea.[52]

The blog won a special Orwell prize in 2009 but the author's cover was broken when *The Times* proposed to name him. The high court refused to grant an injunction protecting his anonymity and the policeman was revealed to be a detective constable in the Lancashire police, Richard Horton. The judge said that blogging was 'essentially a public rather than a private activity' and the public interest would be served by revealing the policeman's identity. There was a cost to Horton when he was given a written warning by his employer, and the blog has been inactive since.[53]

The blogosphere is highly active in specialist areas, such as in the field of wine writing: 'The space devoted to wine and other drink writing in the national press may be dwindling, but nobody seems to have told the bloggers. New wine blogs pop up weekly, conferences take place, bloggers get book deals … '[54] There is a well-worn route for blogs to become books, and a good example in the area of fashion is the Sartorialist blog, started by Scott Schuman in 2005. He began the blog with the idea of 'creating a two-way dialogue about the world of fashion and its relationship to daily life'. He writes about – and posts photographs of – examples of fashion he spots in the street; he also now works for major fashion magazines. Penguin published an anthology of his images in 2009, which sold over 100,000 copies.[55] Blogs can intrigue as well, such as the anonymous diary of a London call girl – *Belle du Jour* – which first appeared in 2003. It won a *Guardian* award for the best-written blog, and one of the judges said that its author was:

> definitely manipulating the blog medium, word by word, sentence by sentence far more effectively than her competitors. It's not merely the titillating striptease aspects that are working for her, but her willingness to use this new form of vanity publishing to throw open a great big global window on activities previously considered unmentionable … She is in a league by herself as a blogger.[56]

The blogger was eventually revealed as Dr Brooke Magnanti, a scientist who listed her interests on her web page as whisky, forensic biometrics, and evidence-based policy.[57] She has since published *Belle du Jour* titles as well as a book about the myths surrounding sex.

Growing in popularity is the use of microblogging tools such as Twitter. By 2012 there were 140 million active users worldwide, posting up to 140 characters with each update. By contrast to YouTube, on which only 1 per cent of users posted content, 60 per cent of users of Twitter had tweeted a message or posted a picture. The popularity of Twitter has been fuelled by the growing penetration of smartphones. Tweets and blog posts are shared on other social networking sites such as Facebook. There have been experiments with fiction on Twitter, and in 2012 Jennifer Egan tweeted a new story, 'The Black Box', in instalments issued

18 The democratization of authorship

over a period of ten days. The bulletins were planned out in a notebook, in handwriting, and the tweets (totalling 8,500 words) were collected together as the complete story in *The New Yorker*.[58]

Blogs and microblogs contribute to a more open ecosystem in which anybody can become an author, but books still offer a route to potential earnings and greater permanence. A book also offers the author something different, the opportunity to develop a narrative or argument over a considerable distance. Steven Johnson contrasts a non-fiction book with a blog, arguing that the former gives you a fully fledged worldview. 'When you visit someone's weblog, you get a wonderful – and sometimes wonderfully intimate – sense of their voice. But when you immerse yourself in a book, you get a different sort of experience: you enter the author's mind, and peer out at the world through their eyes.'[59] In the same way, the novel gives the reader an inner vista which is unparalleled in other media, a first-person experience of other human beings.

What next?

As we have seen, there are many new avenues for authors to take, if they want to find a readership, or have their work published. The digital world has democratized authorship. Anyone can be a writer and potentially reach a global audience, whether by putting an ebook up on Amazon or starting a blog. The only question remaining is whether they have anything interesting to say. The filtering of content may now take place after a work has been made openly available, with readers contributing to the process of deciding quality.

The arrival of the ebook, if seen as just another format alongside the hardback and the paperback, offers advantages to authors. For the novelist Lindsey Davis, 'whereas I once had keen readers who would buy the hardback to look good on the shelf, and buy the paperback to read to destruction, they will now also, if I am very lucky, buy the ebook to have on their Kindle. There is evidence that my readers are doing that.'[60] Digital offers the potential to get much greater connectedness during the writing process itself. Authors can keep in touch with their audiences whilst writing their books and obtain feedback on material and plotlines. They can have access to real-time sales data, for example through Amazon, to help determine which of their books demands a sequel. They can ask their readers to suggest or vote on the best title for their work; and fans can see on a dashboard display how many words of their next work have been written. Given access to the data now being gathered by ebook sellers, authors would have the opportunity to check up on how their books are being read, and gain feedback on which pages are skipped and which passages cause their readers to linger.

Not all will want to take such an interactive approach to their writing, but it does take the promotional aspect of the writer's work back to the very creation of the work. If a potential reader has been involved early on, they will be more likely to buy the final product. Take the example of Imogen Heap, the pop singer and songwriter, who has developed a very close relationship with her fans:

During the production of Heap's ... album *Ellipse*, she regularly published a video-blog in which she discussed the development of her musical ideas. Eventually she published forty video episodes on YouTube during the two years the album was in production. In each episode she played pieces of her music, explained her thinking and asked for feedback. About 50,000 fans regularly followed the blog and commented on what they saw. Heap picked up these comments, entered into a conversation with her fans using different types of digital channels, such as Twitter and Facebook, and allowed the feedback to influence her creative process.[61]

In 2010 the author and marketing guru Seth Godin announced that he was no longer interested in publishing a conventional book. He writes a post for his blog every day, and has built up a wide and interested audience. He believes he can reach many more people through digital means rather than by writing a conventional book. His aim is not to make a profit from his blog, but then he does have a separate and flourishing career as a commentator and speaker. His views on the publishing industry are outspoken:

> The book industry does a great, fabulous, miraculous job of doing what they needed to do in 1965. Great jobs for good people. Ethics that matter. Good taste. Products to be proud of. In terms of responding to changes in the world, I'm at a loss to think of one thing the book industry does well in 2010 that it wasn't already doing in 1990. Not one new thing done well. ... while I'm not sure what form my writing will take, I'm not planning on it being the 1907 version of hardcover publishing any more.[62]

Publishers would say that this is a bit rich coming from somebody who has a number of successful books behind him, which continue to sell. Perhaps he doesn't need to write any more books? But his evangelizing for digital communication is very powerful, as is his belief in the virality of ideas. Shortly afterwards he launched the Domino project, in association with Amazon, with the aim of helping a cadre of high-quality authors to reach a market with books about ideas. Using the domino effect, the ideas would spread from person to person. The books would be quick into the market, and the format agnostic – ebook, audio, but also hardcover. The project was suspended in 2012, with Godin claiming it as a success.

Pierre Bourdieu saw an opposition between two different systems of production of cultural goods. On the one side, there are producers aiming at an audience of their peers, who are also producers of such products. This was reflected in the salon culture in many countries. On the other, there are those aiming to reach the public at large – the non-producers of cultural goods:

> Intellectuals and artists always look suspiciously – though not without a certain fascination – at dazzlingly successful works and authors, sometimes to the extent of seeing worldly failure as a guarantee of salvation in the hereafter:

20 The democratization of authorship

> among other reasons for this, the interference of the 'general public' is such
> that it threatens the field's claims to a monopoly of cultural consecration.[63]

However, some time ago this distinction broke down, with the rules of the market coming, at least in some countries, to apply to literary fiction. Also the new dimensions of authorship today bring the possibility of anyone becoming an author, and reaching markets and audiences in unforeseen ways. Many authors would like to be read as widely as possible.

By and large the ecosystem of fan fiction, social media, and collaborative literature operates in a different world to that of the traditional book. Online writing has generated its own genres, from curtainfic to grave robbery. But the worlds can and do intersect, when say a book publisher picks up a successful blog and turns it into a book, or fan fiction hits the mainstream, as with *Fifty Shades of Grey*. Anonymity may offer some advantages to bloggers, but for book authors who need to enhance their sales by appearances in the media and at festivals, there is mostly no benefit. As part of the shift from author production to author promotion, they need to put themselves out there – that is now part of the job. Their readers want to know more about them, perhaps even meet them at a literary festival. Some will regard this as unfortunate, but there are tools available, such as social media, which facilitate a direct connection with their readers.

We have to return then to why on earth many people still want to write a book – it is mostly for love, not money. Making a living from writing cannot be guaranteed, and the evidence is that the high rewards only accrue to a minority of authors. Whilst John Grisham and James Patterson have the drive to turn themselves into bestselling authors, other authors are writing for the pure pleasure in the process and their achievement. Some authors know they have to write, and may have known this since childhood. Writing fulfils their need for self-actualization, just as an artist has to paint or a musician must make music.[64] There is admiration and reputation attached to being an author; and there is value in a book which people respect and cherish. And it lasts, even beyond the death of the author, past the time when a blog has been discontinued or taken down. As the blogger Maria Popova says, 'Much of what is published online is content designed to be dead within hours.'[65] There is no reason why an ebook cannot last as well, given the right form of conservation, but up until now it is the printed book which has provided a permanence not found in other forms of communication.

Why do authors still want publishers when so many other routes to readers have opened up?[66] They may just want to write, and are less interested in the business and marketing activities. John Locke, a successful self-published author, spends a good part of his time marketing his books. Publishers offer belief, encouragement, and validation of a writer's work – this still works for many readers as well. There may be investment from the publisher forthcoming in terms of an advance or royalty – money upfront to fund time for writing and research – alongside editing and design work, marketing, and the production of printed stock. Also many non-fiction projects originate from publishers, who then approach an author.

What do writers do? As S. J. Watson, author of *Before I Go to Sleep*, says:

> Writers write. They don't sit around thinking all day, or lounge about in their pyjamas with a bowl of Coco Pops, watching daytime television while they wait for the muse to descend (though a little bit of that is permissible) ... you're on your own. Just you and a pen, your courage, and the whole world of your imagination. It's terrifying, and exhilarating.[67]

Notes

1 *Guardian*, 22 February 2010.
2 Neill Denny, then editor of *The Bookseller*, interviewed by Toby Walne, 14 March 2011, thisismoney.co.uk. Available at http://www.thisismoney.co.uk/money/article-1715176/Could-you-become-the-next-big-author.html, accessed 23 September 2013.
3 See Mary Ann Gillies, *The Professional Literary Agent in Britain 1880–1920*, University of Toronto Press, 2007.
4 William Cloonan and Jean-Philippe Postel, 'Literary Agents and the Novel in 1996', *The French Review*, 70:6 (1997), May, page 796.
5 Littell was interviewed by Samuel Blumenfeld, *Le Monde des Livres*, 25 February 2009. The text is taken from thekindlyones.wordpress.com, accessed 27 January 2012.
6 Martin Kretschmer and Philip Hardwick, *Authors' Earnings from Copyright and Non-copyright Sources: A survey of 25,000 British and German writers*, Centre for Intellectual Property Policy & Management, Bournemouth University, December 2007.
7 Author survey by the Writers' Workshop, posted 24 May 2012. Available at http://www.writersworkshop.co.uk/blog/author-survey-the-data/, accessed 14 November 2012.
8 Louis Menand, 'Show or Tell: Should creative writing be taught?', *New Yorker*, 8 June 2009.
9 'Can You Teach Creative Writing?', *Guardian*, 10 May 2011.
10 John Locke, *How I sold 1 Million eBooks in 5 months*, Telemachus Press, 2011.
11 Interviewed by Tim Masters, 'How Wool set Hugh Howey on the road to Hollywood', BBC website, 7 March 2013. Available at http://www.bbc.co.uk/news/entertainment-arts-21674019, accessed 13 March 2013.
12 Dave Cornford and Steven Lewis, *Not a Gold Rush*, Taleist Self-Publishing Survey, 2012.
13 Interviewed by the author, 13 March 2013.
14 Interviewed by the author, 19 November 2012.
15 From her blog, 3 and 22 March 2011, 'Some things need to be said'; 'UPDATED: What I can say right now', amandahocking.blogspot.com.
16 J. K. Rowling, interviewed by Decca Aitkenhead in the *Guardian*, 22 September 2012.
17 Michael Kelley, 'J. K. Rowling to Sell Harry Potter Ebooks from New Website', *The Bookseller*, 23 June 2011.
18 Julie Bosman, 'Best-Selling Author Gives Away His Work', *New York Times*, 26 September 2011.
19 Toby Walne, 'Could You become the Next Big Author?', thisismoney.co.uk, accessed 27 January 2012.
20 Juliet Gardiner, '"What is an Author?" Contemporary publishing discourse and the author figure', *Publishing Research Quarterly*, Spring (2000), page 69.
21 John Updike, 'The End of Authorship', *New York Times*, 25 June 2006.
22 Hemingway was unable to be present so the speech was delivered by John C. Cabot, United States Ambassador to Sweden. Available at http://www.nobelprize.org/nobel_prizes/literature/laureates/1954/hemingway-speech.html, accessed 11 July 2012.
23 Nicholas Wroe, 'John Grisham: A life in writing', *Guardian*, 25 November 2011.
24 Adam Higginbotham, interview with James Patterson, *Daily Telegraph*, 27 January 2010.

22 The democratization of authorship

25 Jon Henley, 'Salman Rushdie's Twitter Debut', *Guardian* blog, 20 September 2011.
26 See http://twitter.com/TouchingTheVoid/ – tweets from May 2012, accessed 11 July 2012.
27 'Mountaineer Laughs Off Twitter Row with "Spotty Schoolkids"', *Guardian*, 24 May 2012.
28 Grace Bello, 'Wattpad Revolutionizes Online Storytelling', *Publishers Weekly*, 21 December 2012.
29 Carolyn Kellogg, 'Amazon launches project to monetize fan fiction: Kindle Worlds', *Los Angeles Times*, 22 May 2013.
30 Grace Westcott, 'Friction over Fan Fiction: Is this burgeoning art form legal?', *Literary Review of Canada*, online original, accessed 3 February 2012.
31 Anik LaChev, 'Fan Fiction: A genre and its (final?) frontiers', *Spectator* 25:1 (2005), Spring, page 84.
32 Henry Jenkins, *Textual Poachers: Television fans and participatory culture*, Routledge, 1992, page 18.
33 Anahad O'Connor and Anemona Hartocollis, 'J. K. Rowling, in Court, Assails Potter Lexicon', *New York Times*, 14 April 2008.
34 See http://www.hp-lexicon.org/index-2-text.html, accessed 20 May 2013.
35 See http://www.newyorker.com/online/blogs/books/2012/05/fifty-shades-of-grey-the-how-to-class.html, accessed 20 May 2013.
36 www.protagonize.com
37 Scott Kraft, 'He Chose His Own Adventure', *The Day*, 10 October 1981.
38 Interview on Spark, 15 January 2012, www.cbc.ca./spark/, accessed 3 February 2012.
39 Kathryn Schulz, 'A Novel of Flying Machines, Apocalyptics and the San Francisco Internet Boom', review in *The New York Times*, 7 October 2011.
40 Anthony Horowitz, 'The Battle for Books', *Guardian*, 28 February 2012.
41 See http://www.youtube.com/watch?v=– 3McxusO7Y, accessed 20 May 2013.
42 See http://jeremyduns.blogspot.co.uk/2011/11/assassin-of-secrets.html, accessed 20 May 2013.
43 See http://jeremyduns.blogspot.co.uk/2011/11/highway-robbery-mask-of-knowing-in.html, accessed 20 May 2013.
44 Dana Goodyear, 'I Love Novels', *New Yorker*, 22 December 2008.
45 Qidong Yun, 'State vs. Market: A perspective on China's publishing Industry', *Logos*, 24:1 (2013).
46 Figure from Cheng Sanguo, CEO of bookdao.com, interviewed by the author, 15 January 2013.
47 The writer Yang Li, and Fu Chenzhou of China Mobile, interviewed by the author, 11 January 2013.
48 Duncan Poupard, 'Of Tombs, Traps and the Intrepid', *China Daily*, 3 August 2012.
49 Interviewed by the author, 11 January 2013.
50 Clifford Coonan, 'China's Mobile Phones Lead a Reading Revolution', *Irish Times*, 1 January 2011.
51 Amanda Lenhart and Susannah Fox, *Bloggers: A portrait of the internet's new storytellers*, Pew Internet & American Life Project, 19 July 2006.
52 See http://nightjack2.wordpress.com/2008/06/20/the-weight/, accessed 20 May 2013.
53 'Night Jack Blog Detective Issued Written Warning by Police Bosses', *Guardian*, 17 June 2009.
54 Fiona Beckett, 'Wine Blogs are Growing by the Case', *Guardian*, 8 September 2012.
55 http://www.thesartorialist.com/
56 Simon Waldman, 'The Best of British Blogging', *Guardian*, 18 December 2003.
57 See belledejour-uk.blogspot.com, accessed 10 February 2012.
58 Jennifer Egan, 'The Black Box', *New Yorker*, 4 June 2012, page 84.
59 Steven Johnson, *Everything Bad is Good for You*, Allen Lane, 2005, page 186.
60 Interviewed by the author, 19 November 2012.
61 Patrik Wikström, *The Music Industry: Music in the cloud*, Polity, 2009, page 176.

62 Jeff Rivera, 'So what do you do, Seth Godin, Author and Marketing Guru?'. Available at mediabistro.com, 25 August 2010, accessed 20 May 2013.

63 Pierre Bourdieu, 'The Market of Symbolic Goods', in *The Field of Cultural Production: Essays on art and literature*, Columbia University Press, 1984, page 6.

64 See A. H. Maslow, 'A Theory of Human Motivation', *Psychological Review*, 50 (1943), pages 370–96.

65 Interviewed in the *Observer*, 30 December 2012.

66 See, for example, the guide to self-publishing by Alison Baverstock: *The Naked Author*, Bloomsbury, 2011.

67 S. J. Watson, 'What a Creative Writing Course Taught me', *Guardian*, 18 January 2013.

2

SLOW BOOKS

Just as the prospects for books look limited without authors, the same applies without readers. Paul Auster says, 'If you write a story or a poem, you hope there will be a reader,'[1] although of course there are a good many titles read by very few people. There is a received wisdom that reading is good in itself, and offers personal and social benefits beyond those for the economy of having an educated and literate population. If studies show that readership of books is in decline, does this matter? What is at stake here? Are there other ways of learning and developing our intelligence, and how can we expect books to compete with the range of other media which compete for our attention?

Surveys suggest a fall in reading over time, in many countries, and this chapter will examine the evidence and the reasons put forward. These include the loss of time to read, in an often frenetic world of competing demands, and declining interest amongst newer generations. Is the reading of books being replaced by other forms of reading, for example blogs and websites? The science of reading tells us what is happening inside our brains, and suggests that the pace of reading is faster with some digital devices.

Decline in reading

The statistics regarding reading have to be treated with some caution. There is no satisfactory set of data over a long period, and certainly none which can provide watertight comparisons between countries. Since reading books is perceived as a desirable activity some respondents to general surveys may be unwilling to say they read nothing.

The evidence from longitudinal studies of reading suggests that the reading of books has been in decline for some time, stretching back to the dawn of the age of television. The Netherlands is a country with a strong reading culture, and a diary study over the period 1975 to 1990 discovered diminishing levels of reading, due to two main factors. Firstly people's lives had become busier, leaving less time for reading; secondly reading was being replaced by the viewing of television. Cohorts in the study which had grown up before the advent of television were likely to remain loyal to reading. Examining the period between 1975 and 2000, an overview impression would suggest that there had been no decline in reading in the Netherlands, since general surveys suggested that the proportion of the population reading for pleasure remained just over 50 per cent. A more detailed examination of reading habits in one particular week (the same week in 1975 and 2000) showed that whilst 49 per cent reported reading books (outside of work or education) for at least 15 minutes in the course of a week in October in 1975, the figure had fallen to 31 per cent in an October week in 2000.[2]

The work by John P. Robinson and Geoffrey Godbey on time-use data in the USA shows that it is hard to generalize over long periods of time – trends do not necessarily persist. Firstly their work echoes a finding from the Dutch studies, with television taking time away from reading books. In 1965 those without a television were devoting 14 minutes a day to reading books, by comparison to TV owners who were spending around 8 minutes a day. But looking forward to the 1980s, reading remained a 'resilient free-time activity' – time spent reading books and magazines had actually risen, compensating for a fall in newspaper reading. Cohort analysis showed that almost all age groups had increased their reading time as they aged between the years of the study (1965 to 1985).

> While one could lament the fact that only one-sixth as much total time is devoted to reading as to television [in 1985], people do seem to increase their reading time as they age. In particular, women continue to be particularly supportive of or reliant on this 'obsolete' form of leisure activity.[3]

The overall analysis showed that while people may subjectively have felt more rushed, they had in general gained more free time. Over the period from the 1960s to the 1990s, most of the gain in free time in the adult population (4.5 hours per week for women, 7.9 hours for men) had been taken up by television. There was a modest decline in the overall figure for reading (including magazines and newspapers), from 3.0 hours to 2.8 hours per week. In the final decade under review, the gain in free time was not wholly given over to television and, for example, men were spending some of the extra time on a new device, the computer, or in fitness activities. The authors concluded that the data was not yet showing up the effect of computer use on other activities, but already they could see that computer users demonstrated higher usage of print and other media.

There appears to be a definite cohort effect which may buck longer-term trends around reading. Alarmed by the launch of Sputnik by the USSR in 1957, the US government ploughed funds into research and education, which in turn stimulated higher levels of publishing output. As the baby boomers of this period had children, books for children took off as a profitable sector of book publishing. The

26 Slow books

impact of the Sputnik factor on literacy levels is still being felt, and 'to this day, baby boomers buy books in greater proportions than the rest of the population ... [they] are also inclined to buy books for professional development, which seems to mirror the emphasis on knowledge dissemination so intense during their childhood.'[4]

The US National Endowment for the Arts has been surveying participation in the arts on a regular basis, and caused a stir with the publication in 2004 of its report on *Reading at Risk*.[5] This concluded that over a 20-year period, literary reading in America had not only declined rapidly among all groups, but the rate of decline had accelerated, especially among the young. Indeed the percentage of the population reading any books declined from 60.9 per cent in 1992 to 56.6 per cent in 2002. The disturbing findings of the report were ameliorated to some extent by a follow-up report, *Reading on the Rise*, published in 2009, which now highlighted an increase in literary reading among adult Americans.[6] Reversing a declining trend, there was a 'decisive and unambiguous' increase among virtually every group measured. The percentage of 18- to 24-year-olds who had read literature had grown by nearly 9 points, representing 3.4m additional readers.

In China there appears to be a cohort effect of more young people reading, amongst those who have benefited from the greater educational opportunities since the 1980s. Middle-aged people find it hard to read books for entertainment as they may feel stretched for time by a range of responsibilities, from getting on at work to looking after their children or parents, and will read newspapers, magazines, or content online. By contrast young people in their twenties have the time to read books, and the literary agent Jackie Huang says, 'The main readers in China are young people. They read many books, but at thirty years old, when they get married, everything changes.'[7]

A longitudinal study, published in 2007, in several countries (the Netherlands, Norway, France, UK, and USA), examined reading as a primary activity – outside work or education – and discovered a complex picture.[8] The study examined reading of all print materials: books, newspapers, and magazines. In the UK, for the period 1975 to 2000, the study discovered that despite a decline in participation rates (from 66 to 58 per cent), those who did read were spending more time on the activity. In France there was also a decline in participation, in the period 1974 to 1998, from 44 per cent to 35 per cent – but a small increase in the time spent. In Norway both participation rates and time spent had increased.

> Arguably, concern regarding de-reading (as measured according to the duration of time allocated to the practice) is misplaced in all countries except the USA, where reductions of time spent reading leaves a small minority of its population engaging in the practice. Dereading in the Netherlands is evident, however this is a country with a very strong reading tradition and despite decline of time spent in the practice still is the country where reading remains most widespread. In France, the UK and Norway reading is on the rise, although in France and the UK this is book as opposed to magazine and newspaper reading.[9]

The authors found a mildly healthy picture when it came to book reading, with small increases in both participation rates and time spent. The authors suggested that the figures could be revealing the emergence of a reading class, 'a highly educated group of committed practitioners who value book reading as a form of social distinction'.[10]

A similar study today would wish to include use of digital devices alongside the reading of print materials in general. Using a definition of reading which includes our use of the internet, it is estimated that we spend three times as much time reading as we did in 1980.[11] The General Lifestyle Survey in the UK first asked about ownership of a home computer in 1984, and since then the proportion of households with a home computer has increased consistently from just over one in eight households in 1985 to eight in ten households in 2011.[12] One estimate suggests that, taking into account both print and computer usage, the average American reads an astonishing 35,000 words a day.[13] We are also writing more as part of our daily lives, from emailing and texting to our interactions through social media.

Research into the use of text messaging by pre-teen children found a positive correlation between the use of textisms (text language abbreviations) and their phonetic abilities, and no deleterious effects on literacy skills. 'Word reading ability and performance on the Spoonerism test [a test of phonological awareness] were found to be significantly associated with the age at which children received their first mobile phone and with the proportion of textisms used in their text messages.'[14] There exists a further body of research which shows a connection between phonological awareness – awareness of the sound structure of spoken words – and reading attainment.

James Flynn is well known for the 'Flynn effect', the documentation of substantial IQ gains from one generation to another. He believes that we now live in a time which poses 'a wider range of cognitive problems than our ancestors encountered' and so have developed 'new cognitive skills and the kind of brains that can deal with these problems'.[15] In his analysis of IQ tests in the USA, he discovered a growing gap between the vocabulary of adults and children. Between 1950 and 2004, the gain in American adults in their active vocabulary was four times greater than that found amongst schoolchildren. He argues that this is due to the changing workplace; and that rising numbers in tertiary education played a part indirectly by helping to change the kind of jobs being done, for example in professional and managerial roles. In the workplace, there are now more talkers and fewer listeners and this has encouraged the development of vocabulary skills. By contrast in the area of passive vocabulary, American adults have made much lower gains – for example in a test which discovers 'what words people are likely to understand in context if someone else uses them or if they read them in a book'.[16] Overall the gains in adult vocabulary open up a larger target audience for books, but he thinks today's visual culture limits the numbers willing to read.

In the case of children, he finds that although they may master basic reading skills at a younger age, they are 'no better prepared for reading more demanding adult literature. You cannot enjoy War and Peace if you have to run to the

28 Slow books

dictionary or encyclopedia every other paragraph'.[17] Indeed he sees a divide between adults and children which has opened up, and that children cannot necessarily understand their parents or answer them in their vocabulary. Teenagers have their own sub-culture and vocabulary level. Although this does not do much harm in the long run, since the effect is levelled out when they enter the world of work, it is surprising to see how little vocabulary gain has happened amongst American schoolchildren over a long period. The development of a sub-culture can also go towards explaining the growth of teen fiction as a separate genre.

International differences

There are variations in reading between different countries but by and large reading tends to correlate with income and levels of education. Life stages are also important, and during the time when people are most preoccupied with young children, there is often simply less time to read. Overall women read more than men, and the gap appears to be widening.

Looking at participation in reading across the whole European Union in 2007, 71 per cent of people had read a book at least once in the previous 12 months. The percentage who had read more than five books was 37 per cent, and the percentage who had read no books was 28 per cent. Worthy of note was that participation in reading was highest amongst the youngest age group surveyed (15–24) and lowest amongst the oldest age group (55+). Participation also increased according to the degree of urbanization, with the highest rates found in large towns rather than in smaller towns or villages. The Eurobarometer survey found differences between countries. In the top countries for reading at least one book in the previous 12 months were Sweden (87 per cent), the Netherlands (84 per cent), and Denmark (83 per cent). For those reading more than five books in the previous 12 months, the highest averages were found in Sweden (60 per cent), Denmark (56 per cent), and the United Kingdom (56 per cent). The survey also produced figures for those reading no books in the previous year: the highest averages were found in Malta (54 per cent), Portugal (49 per cent), and Cyprus (43 per cent).[18]

The Harmonised European Time Use Survey (HETUS), carried out by several European countries between 1998 and 2006, offers some insights into the national differences between European countries. Respondents to the survey were asked about the time they spent reading books (excluding any reading for study purposes). Other reading could include newspapers and magazines as well as brochures. Overall the contrast with the amount of time spent watching television is pronounced.

Analysis of the time-use data suggests some generalizations about countries and their reading habits and overall leisure time. There are higher levels of reading in northern European countries, for example, by comparison to the Mediterranean countries. It has been suggested that there is less leisure time in the southern

Slow books **29**

TABLE 2.1 Mean time spent per day on reading and watching TV

Country	Reading books (minutes)	Watching TV or video (hours: minutes)	Other reading (minutes)
Estonia	16	2:16	21
Finland	12	2:13	34
Latvia	11	2:05	17
Sweden	11	1:48	21
Poland	10	2:18	13
Norway	9	1:52	27
Lithuania	8	2:16	15
Bulgaria	8	2:27	10
Belgium	7	2:24	19
Germany	7	1:49	31
Slovenia	7	1:57	16
United Kingdom	6	2:23	20
Italy	5	1:40	13
Spain	4	1:53	11
France	1	2:01	22

Source: Harmonised European Time Use Survey (online database version 2.0). Created 2005–2007 by Statistics Finland and Statistics Sweden (reference date 2007-10-01). http://www.tus.scb.se

countries as lunch breaks tend to be longer. Men in all countries tend to have more leisure time than women and devote more of their time to television and video, rather than to other cultural activities.[19]

There are broader cultural and historical influences and we have seen that levels of participation tend to correlate to levels of urbanization. Societies which have retained strong rural economies may have lower levels of participation in reading. Camilla Addey suggests in her study of reading habits in the UK and Italy that an individualistic society is more likely to view reading books in a positive light than one built on collectivist principles. An understanding of why there is a stronger reading habit in the UK than in Italy should take this into account: 'compared to the UK ... Italians tend to converge on group activities such as cooking, eating together, discussing politics, watching TV in public cafes, strolling up and down the main street in the evening ("la passeggiata") and so on.'[20] Does religion also play a part in different traditions around reading? Whilst, traditionally, Protestantism encourages the silent and personal reading of the Bible, Catholicism expects Scriptures to be interpreted by the clergy. Addey argues that:

> The present-day attitudes to reading ... must certainly owe something to these very different religious and historical backgrounds: in the case of readers in the Roman Catholic tradition, there may be an underlying conviction that the spoken word is somehow superior to the written word, whereas people from the Protestant tradition may feel that the written word has an authority lacking in the spoken word.[21]

30 Slow books

A country with a strong tradition of reading books is Finland. Around three-quarters of the population were book readers in 2009, and they spend 45 minutes a day reading, whether books or magazines.[22] This figure has stayed constant for over two decades, and can be attributed to the strong education system. In the PISA 2009 international league table of reading literacy amongst 15-year-olds, Finland came second out of OECD countries, after Korea.[23] It is said that the country is built on wood – with its forests and paper industry – and also its head – through its excellent education system.

Reading is at the heart of the Finnish culture, as was commented on in 2005:

> Eighty-five percent of Finnish families subscribe to a daily newspaper. Only Norwegians and Japanese subscribe at a higher rate. A typical Finnish family starts its day at the breakfast table by reading the morning paper and commenting on the day's news. The number of books published annually in Finland is high given the size of the population, and each Finn borrows 21 library books, on average, each year.
>
> Approximately half of Finnish television broadcasts are in a foreign language. Most programs are in English, but Swedish, German, and French programs are also popular. The programs have Finnish subtitles instead of dubbing, so children need to read even when watching television. They learn to read quickly – favourite television programs are much more motivating than any speed-reading exercises assigned in class.[24]

It is likely that many Finns today read their news off the web, but still Finland has high rates of newspaper readership, ranking third in the world in terms of circulation in relation to its population.[25]

In comparison to Finland, levels of book readership in Greece are low. Research carried out in 2010 by the National Book Centre of Greece showed that just over 40 per cent of the population did not read any books at all, around 44 per cent read from one to nine books a year, and only 8 per cent read ten books or more. Participation in reading was lower amongst younger cohorts of the population. Overall there was an improving picture from a previous survey in 2004, when 44 per cent read no books at all, 34 per cent read more than one book, and again 8 per cent fell into the category of heavy readers.[26] Suggested reasons for the low level of reading culture include the Mediterranean climate, the relatively recent growth of higher education, and the newly emerging role of libraries (usage rates for libraries are the lowest in Europe).[27] Readership of newspapers is also low, with just over 30 per cent of Greeks reading a daily newspaper in 2007.[28]

If there are cultural differences which affect the reading of books, these may be long standing. Over time participation rates are likely to be self-perpetuating, and an OECD report concluded that whilst the reading habits of parents are closely related to their socio-economic status, what influences reading in their children is the habits themselves:

Not surprisingly, in all countries and economies surveyed, children whose parents consider reading a hobby, enjoy going to the library or bookstore, and spend time reading for enjoyment at home are more likely to enjoy reading themselves. This is true even when comparing children from similar socio-economic backgrounds, which indicates that children are more likely to enjoy reading when their home environment is conducive to reading.[29]

A reading class

Mentioned above is the connection between reading books and socio-economic class. As can be seen in Table 2.2, which gives data for the UK, there is a strong stratification between the four main class groups, with only 18 per cent of people in the AB group (managerial and professional) not reading books at all; whilst the figure increases to 43 per cent amongst the C2 and DE groups (including manual and casual workers).

We can relate these differences to income but there are also issues around class itself and the aspirations which are held by different groups. In a 2010 study of engagement with the arts (e.g. visiting the theatre or being a member of a book club), 68 per cent of people from higher socio-economic groups had engaged in the arts at least three times in the previous 12 months. This was 21 percentage points higher than the arts engagement level among those from lower socio-economic groups, at 47 per cent.[30]

These correlations with income and class align with Bourdieu's arguments regarding the acquisition of cultural capital in society. The acquisition of such capital is dependent on both education and family background: 'surveys establish that all cultural practices (museum visits, concert-going, reading etc.), and preferences in literature, painting or music, are closely linked to educational level (measured by qualifications or length of schooling) and secondarily to social origin.'[31] Families higher up in the class system pass on to their children an initial stock of cultural capital. The acquisition of cultural capital is further rewarded in the education system, which is built around high culture and its appreciation, which in turn leads to recruitment into the professional and managerial class.

TABLE 2.2 Demographics for reading books in the UK (%)

Socio-economic group	Non-reader	Light 1–10 minutes per day	Medium 11–30 minutes per day	Heavy Over 30 minutes per day	Total from three previous columns
AB	18	6	21	53	80
C1	29	10	18	44	72
C2	43	10	11	34	55
DE	43	7	10	35	52

Source: Book Marketing Limited, Expanding the Market, 2005. These figures are for reading when not on holiday.

32 Slow books

Writing about Western cultures, Wendy Griswold identifies the emergence of a reading class, avid readers who are part of a communications elite. Typically well educated, affluent, and metropolitan, they exhibit a 'more–more' pattern of cultural participation, and form a self-perpetuating minority. Prestige attaches itself to books, writers, and reading, and society will honour the practice of reading. 'For reading is not just a peculiar form of entertainment for those who can afford it, like playing polo, but a way for powerful people to communicate with one another.'[32]

Similarly, a study of book reading in China found links between education and book reading, with, for example, those with higher levels of education reading a wider range of genres. It also found links between reading habits and social class. Those in authority at their workplace (government/party officials and enterprise managers) and those with professional or administrative skills not only read highbrow books more often but also read significantly more widely across genres than did other groups. Self-employed people read less highbrow books than other social classes, and read less overall than production and service workers. The suggestion was that this group had the least amount of leisure time. Class was observed to have little impact on the reading of popular fiction, despite the fact that this is held in low esteem in Chinese culture. Overall the authors concluded:

> Chinese adults who live in the same city and are matched in gender, age, and education vary in their scope of reading and their reading preferences because they belong to different occupational classes. This means that class distinction, as measured by possession of authority, skill, or property, significantly differentiates reading habits and taste.[33]

The popularity of reading on mobile phones in China occurs amongst a particular class of readers. There are as many men as women, reading the equivalent of the pulp fiction of the 1920s to 1950s in the USA, which then included such genres as crime and science fiction. The Chinese readership is exploring a range of genres from romance through to time travel. There are 100m active users of one mobile reading platform, paying for whole books or by the chapter; and over 200m people reading across mobile and literature websites. The profile of the typical reader is a young person (under the age of 35), with a low level of education and a low income. For example, someone leaving the land and arriving to work in a city, perhaps on a construction site, will not have the money to afford much by way of media. For them low-priced fiction will be attractive entertainment, allowing them to dream of adventure and another life.[34]

The stratification of readers has also been shown clearly in Brazil, where research has tracked reading ability over a ten-year period.[35] As incomes have grown, there has been a modest increase in the percentage of the population in the AB classes, but a significant rise in the percentage of the population in the C class (as defined by monthly income). This change can be mapped in the area of literacy, where there has been a marked decrease in functional illiteracy. The proportions of the

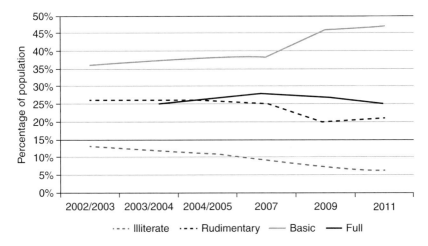

FIGURE 2.1 Literacy rates in Brazil
Source: O Instituto Paulo Montenegro e a ONG Ação Educativa, 2011. © INAF

population with rudimentary literacy, or who are completely illiterate, have fallen. Those with a full level of literacy, capable of reading literary fiction, has remained at a stable 25 per cent of the population, whilst those with a basic level of literacy has risen as a proportion of the population. The latter can read simpler fiction such as *Fifty Shades of Grey* (which was a bestseller in Brazil) but would not feel comfortable in attempting literary fiction. The Brazilian publisher and journalist Carlo Carrenho says:

> The new readers are basic readers, people who will never read the Man Booker Prize winners, but they read very simple self-help. ... The big trend in the last few years is that the readership in Brazil is growing with people from the C class, but also with people who are becoming basic literates, and not full literates as all the high-brow publishers would love them to be.[36]

Competition with other media

If the reading of books is in decline in many countries, is it surprising with the wealth of other media that now compete with books? We have seen how the rise of television has had an impact, but this in turn has faced competition from games and the internet. The mobile phone is a constant companion for many people around the world, as observed by Laura Miller:

> reading competes with many other claims on people's leisure time, and has a hard time prevailing over video games, the internet, mobile phones, DVDs, iPods, and television, not to mention non-media-related activities. Indeed, texting seems to have replaced reading as the default activity for the

34 Slow books

> interstices of daily life – for how people pass the time on public transport or
> in waiting rooms, when lying on the beach or sitting in the park.[37]

We have an increasing ability to multi-task, using a number of media devices
simultaneously, and our playing of video games is creating a highly dextrous and
mentally agile population.

A survey in 2010 revealed that adults in the UK spent 242 minutes daily
watching television on a TV set, up by 23 minutes from 2005, while radio
accounted for 173 minutes per day, down by 22 minutes over the same period.
Internet activities (undertaken on a fixed internet connection, using web and
applications) experienced the largest increase in average daily use, nearly doubling
from 15 minutes in 2005 to 28 minutes in 2010. Of adults, 48 per cent had a social
networking profile, and 32 per cent were using their mobile phone to access the
internet (figures for early 2011).[38]

Over a quarter of adults owned a smartphone, and this was having an impact on
other aspects of life. Those surveyed suggested they were doing less of the following now they had a smartphone: taking photos with a camera (16%), using a
PC to access the internet (15%), reading a printed newspaper (13%), using a paper
map (13%), watching TV (10%), playing games on a console/PC (7%), socializing
with friends (4%), and taking part in sport (4%). Amongst adults, 9 per cent said
they were reading books less; the figure was 15 per cent amongst teenagers.[39]

Research into the millennial generation – those born after 1980 – suggests a
substitution effect between books and social media. So-called 'restrained millennials', who showed the least interest in social media, were the most active book
readers. By contrast the clusters who used social media the most were also those
who read books the least often. As usage of social media increases, and becomes
more active (rather than simply as a passive recipient of content), the gender profile
shifts more towards males. This mirrors the higher amount of book reading
observed amongst female readers.[40]

The proliferation of devices is also changing the way we consume media, with
people viewing TV and video through the internet and on mobile phones.
Estimates from 2012 suggest that between 10 and 15 per cent of all video content
was viewed on internet-connected devices.[41] Media meshing, consuming two
media simultaneously, is growing as an activity. TV viewers may consult the
internet on another device whilst watching a programme, for example to find out
more about the actor they are watching, or discuss the show with their friends on
social media. During the screening of the Super Bowl in 2011, rankings of tweets
showed heavily increased activity around the brands being advertised during com-
mercials. After Doritos ads appeared, the brand started to appear high up in the global
Twitter rankings. 'Meshing satisfies the consumer's need for immediate gratification
to a query or concern. It also creates an interesting dynamic, where offline media
acts as a trigger for online behaviours.'[42]

If we look at computer and video games, 72 per cent of households in the USA
in 2011 played games. The average age of the player was 37, with 18 per cent of

Slow books **35**

players under 18, 53 per cent between 18 and 49, and 29 per cent over 50. The gender balance was 58 per cent male, 42 per cent female. Some of the top reasons for purchasing a game were the quality of the graphics, an interesting storyline, a sequel to a favourite game, and word of mouth.[43]

Of the time spent online, around 40 per cent is spent on three activities: social networking, gaming, and emailing.[44] As Dennis Baron writes:

> it's not simply a lack of fresh air and sunshine, it's the quality – more specifically, the perceived lack of quality – of the digital interaction that provokes some critics, who dismiss the time we spend reading and writing on screen as time wasted on the trivia of IM, email, or web surfing. It's time taken away not just from face-to-face interaction, but also from reading and writing what the critics consider more worthwhile texts, or engaging in salon-quality conversations.[45]

Readers are also the next generation of authors, and the novelist Lindsey Davis ponders the risks of a highly visual world of media:

> I am old enough to be part of the radio generation. I want the words. I don't want to see it; I can see it in my head. ... Long term there is a possibility – I am not saying it will definitely happen – that the kind of creative imagination that led to good novels being produced won't exist because children won't be brought up to have that kind of imagination.[46]

Ereading

Is the popularity of new reading devices likely to have an impact on reading habits? There is no consistent set of data which we can use to track any changes, but there are some interesting trends developing. Ereading seems to encourage rather than discourage reading, although there are differences across devices and there may be a positive effect in the short term from the novelty of the devices.

A 2012 study in the USA, the most advanced market for purchasing and reading ebooks, showed that the availability of ebooks was encouraging reading. Those who read ebooks reported reading more books in all formats. They read an average of 24 books over a year, whilst those who did not read ebooks read an average of 15 books. Owners of dedicated ereaders again read an average of 24 books over the year, against 16 books for those who did not own such a device. New devices were encouraging reading, with 41 per cent of tablet owners and 35 per cent of ereader owners reading more since the advent of digital content. Over 40 per cent of readers of ebooks said they were reading more.[47]

Digital reading has the potential to broaden the base of readers of books. For example in China there is no strong reading culture as there is in some Western countries. Families do not have many books displayed at home, and often there is not the space in small apartments to create libraries of printed books. The book market for general titles is still developing, and as Jackie Huang says:

36 Slow books

> Ebooks change the way of reading, and more and more poor people can read on their mobile, they can read on their computer – the ebook gives the Chinese people a new way of reading much faster – suddenly they are so convenient. You can buy online and the book is cheaper than the printed copy.[48]

Intuitively the advantage of reading a printed book is that it is not a screen. We spend so much of our working life using a screen, surely it is a relief to switch to another form of media? But there has come a point where ereading devices have improved so much that they can offer a degree of superiority for some people, and this is especially the case for dedicated ereaders. First, their screens no longer cause the eye strain encountered from reading on PCs; some can be read in full sunlight, whilst others are backlit, facilitating reading in bed when your partner is asleep. Second, there have been significant gains in battery life, so the risk is minimized of having to recharge your device at some exciting point in the plot of a thriller. Third, there are advantages to having the portability of an ereader which can carry many books – whether for travel or commuting. Those readers with several books on the go can also choose the title to suit their mood. Having a portable device means you can fill in those gaps of time in the day, whether waiting outside the school gates or having a coffee before a meeting. Fourth, with an ereader you can vary the type size (and font) to match your own preference or the quality of your eyesight. Fifth, there is a range of possible additional functionality, which includes a measure of your reading speed, the opportunity to see who else around the world is reading the same title at the same time, and the ability to tweet your reading choices to your friends and family.

What is striking, however, is how, to become successful, ereaders have had to mimic the styling of dead tree products – including their look and feel, and how pages are turned. As an example of such skeuomorphic design, reading on an iPad simulates reading physical books, from the wooden bookshelf which holds your books to the action of turning pages. You can swipe your finger to turn to the next page, and see it reveal itself. In a similar way, taking a photo on an iPhone can mimic the sound of the shutter on an SLR camera. In any case reading on electronic devices has moved ahead so far that it has now come to mimic the *lean back* technology of the printed book (as opposed to the *lean forward* technology of the PC).[49]

Is reading on screen a different experience to reading a print book? We can view this in different ways, from how it feels to the efficiency of the act. Anne Mangen speaks for many people when she contrasts the experience of digital reading to reading a print book. She concentrates on the experience of hypertext fiction – digital texts which offer hyperlinks and other forms of navigation through the story – and compares this to the immersive experience of a print novel. She regards the degree of immersion as dependent on the very materiality of the print pages:

> The feeling of literally being in touch with the text is lost when your actions – clicking with the mouse, pointing on touch screens or scrolling

with keys or on touch pads – take place at a distance from the digital text, which is, somehow, somewhere inside the computer, the e-book or the mobile phone. ... The print text is tangible – it is physically, tactilely, graspable, in ways that digital texts are not (until they are printed out and hence no longer digital).[50]

A study at Princeton in 2009 introduced the Kindle to students and examined their attitudes to using the new device. Students liked the portability and weight of the device, the legibility of the screen, the battery life, and the search facility. They did remark, however, that it was difficult to assess the length of what they were reading: 'no one seemed able to internalize the concept of the Kindle "locations" to the same degree that they were already familiar with the concept of "pages".'[51] The students were primarily using the device in their studies, and the pilot achieved one of its main objectives, with the group printing out half the quantity of material compared to the control groups. Even so, many participants in the pilot did not feel that the ereader was as useful for annotations as using paper. One participant said: 'I loved the Kindle for readings that I didn't have to annotate extensively'; another commented 'I think it's great for pleasure reading, not good for study reading.'[52]

Another qualitative study, undertaken amongst graduate students at a library school in New York, again found enthusiasm for the Kindle.[53] There was a reported increase in reading compared to the use of printed books. The participants mostly read books whilst at home or commuting, and they found the portability and convenience of the Kindle to be a significant plus:

It's incredibly easy to read and carry the Kindle around. ... It's remarkably easy to read on the device even standing and holding the strap on the subway, noticeably easier than with a hardcover book. Sometimes when I am on a lunch break I realize that I would like to have pulled out the book I am currently reading but it's stuck at home.[54]

Amongst the categories of books they thought suitable for an ereader were short books and 'fast' fiction. The experience of reading was considered as immersive as with a printed book, and one participant said they seemed to be reading faster than with print.

Early studies which compared reading on screen to reading on paper, dating back as far as the 1980s, in general showed that paper produced higher performance levels with regard to comprehension, accuracy, and speed.[55] But these were using early screens and displays, and it was often difficult to provide a satisfactory equivalence. Improvements in screen displays and the introduction of dedicated reading devices now offer the chance to assess what differences there are, if any. Certainly the on-screen reading experience has improved markedly, with easily portable devices which do not give the reader eye strain.

In a 2011 study carried out in Germany, participants were divided into two sample groups, one with an average age of 26, the other with an average age of

38 Slow books

64.[56] Each participant read various texts with different levels of complexity on an ebook reader (Kindle), a tablet computer (iPad), and paper. The reading behaviour of the participants and their corresponding neural processes were assessed using measures of eye movements (eye tracking) and electrophysiological brain activity (EEG). 'Almost all of the participants stated that they liked reading a printed book best. This was the dominant subjective response, but it does not match the data obtained from the study,' said Professor Matthias Schlesewsky of the Johannes Gutenberg University Mainz. The participants said that they preferred reading from a printed book, but the performance tests showed that there was no difference between reading from a printed book and on the ereader. Further, the study found that tablet computers provide an advantage over ereaders and the printed page that is not consciously perceivable. Whilst there were no differences between the three devices in terms of rates of reading by the younger participants, the older participants exhibited faster reading times when using the tablet.

A separate study, carried out in the USA in 2012, showed that reading on a back-lit tablet improved reading speeds amongst a range of subjects with different levels of eyesight. There was a significant improvement in the reading speed amongst those with poor vision, and the researchers suggested that the tablet provided a higher degree of contrast for words. In terms of comfort, subjects with poor vision found the tablet the most comfortable reading experience, whilst readers with good vision preferred print.[57] The arrival of ebooks provides significant benefits to the visually impaired reader, who can adjust the text size or make use of text-to-speech functionality.

The science of reading

The relatively new science of reading informs our understanding of the process of reading, and helps to identify the benefits.

The process of reading begins with the eye. The part of the eye we use for reading is the central area, the fovea, taking up around 15 per cent of our visual field. This has cells sensitive to incoming light, which have the resolution we need to read letters. In order to read we have to move our eyes across the page, ensuring that words come into the field of view of the fovea. Our eyes do not move smoothly but in small steps called saccades. Given this set-up, it is not necessarily true that larger characters are easy to read, since they may move words to the periphery of the retina. This is, however, within the limitations of a person's overall eyesight, which may mean that some letters are just too small and that an increase in type size will be beneficial.

A single view of the words on a page can only take in a small number of characters, and our brain is set up to move our eyes along the line by about seven to nine letters at a time. What is astonishing is that in accomplished readers, the visual system can process all the letters in a word in parallel, regardless of the number of letters (within some boundaries, roughly from three to eight letters). The visual form of a letter string is then identified in the left-hand side of the brain, in the left occipito-temporal area – what the neuroscientist Stanislas Dehaene calls the 'brain's letterbox'. The visual information is then distributed to other parts of the left hemisphere, which encode the meaning of words, sound pattern, and articulation.

> A written or spoken word probably activates fragments of meaning in the brain in much the same way that a tidal bore invades a whole riverbed. If you compare a word like 'cheese' with a non-word like 'croil,' the only difference lies in the size of the cortical tidal wave that they can bring on. A known word resonates in the temporal lobe networks and produces a massive wave of synchronized oscillations that rolls through millions of neurons. This tidal bore goes even as far as the more distant regions of the cortex as it successively contacts the many assemblies of neurons that each encode a fragment of the word's meaning. An unknown word, however, even if it gets through the first stages of visual analysis, finds no echo in the cortex and the wave it triggers is quickly broken down into inarticulate cerebral foam.[58]

Scientists can now track the speed of this wave of cerebral activity: for example, in the first 150 milliseconds of reading a simple word, activity is restricted to the visual cortex, and at around 200 milliseconds, the left letterbox area is activated.

What Dehaene concluded is that our brains are not naturally adapted to reading, but that the circuitry inherited from our primate beginnings have been co-opted to the task of recognizing printed words. 'Our neuronal networks are literally "recycled" for reading.'[59] It is not a question of the evolution of the brain, but of reading evolving to work in conjunction with our brain circuits. Writing structures have been designed with a set of shapes which are simple enough so that it only takes a few years for the systems to invade the neuronal circuits of the learner. Dehaene believes that 'the cultural form of writing systems must have evolved in accordance with the brain's learnability constraints, converging progressively on a small set of symbol shapes that can be optimally learned by these particular visual areas.'[60]

Reading does still impact on our brains. In a study published in 1998, researchers concluded that learning to read and write during childhood influences the functional organization of the adult human brain.[61] The brains were scanned of two groups of Portuguese adults: one literate, one illiterate. The illiterate group had never been to school, and had no knowledge of reading or writing. The participants were asked to repeat both real Portuguese words and pseudo-words. Although the two groups had comparable vocabulary banks, the illiterate group had difficulty when it came to repeating the pseudo-words. The difference was consistent with the hypothesis that the absence of knowledge of orthography was limiting the ability of the illiterate subjects to repeat the pseudo-words correctly, and this was related to a failure to activate an adequately configured neural network. The research revealed that readers had developed new language processing

40 Slow books

possibilities, with brain imaging showing that readers had more developed brains – the literate group engaged many more resources in the left hemisphere.

A more recent study used brain imaging to show changes in blood flow levels to many areas of the brain during reading, demonstrating the neural complexity and potential cognitive benefits of literary study. Subjects were asked to read from *Mansfield Park* by Jane Austen in two different manners: they alternated between reading the text for pleasure, and giving the text a close reading for literary analysis (participants were PhD students familiar with reading a text for plot, characterization, and tone). The results for close reading showed 'unbelievably widespread changes in brain activity' for many of the individuals, as estimated from averaged changes in blood flow. This suggests that the level – and kind – of attention we give to a text is important, and the key influence may be 'not just what we read, but how we read'. Blood flow increased not only during close reading, but also in unique regions during pleasure reading, and the research lead, Natalie Phillips from Michigan State University, says 'there is also a different neural signature, or a distinctive set of brain regions, being activated during pleasure reading'. Not only do the regions activated for close reading extend far beyond those traditionally associated with directed attention, the regions involved in relaxed reading reach far beyond the brain's pleasure centres. Her study suggests that the type of attention we bring to reading is important, and that various forms of reading may in fact influence and enhance the development of cognitive and neural flexibility.

> In fact, if we would like to use the most regions of our brain, sum total, reading both for study and for pleasure is the key. Moreover, reading is far more complex than we could have imagined, producing a wider activation of brain regions than we would ever have thought.[62]

Scientists are also beginning to show how the brain links our reading of words to our memory and imagination. In a 2009 study, brain imaging showed how neural systems track changes in the situation described by a story.[63] Participants in the study were given MRI scans whilst they read simple stories with characters, objects, and goals. Different brain regions were shown to track different aspects of a story, such as a character's physical location or current goals. Regions involved in processing goal-directed human activity, navigating spatial environments, and manipulating objects in the real world increased in activation at points when those specific aspects of the narrated situation were changing. Overall the researchers concluded that the results were consistent with the idea that readers construct simulations of situations as they read a text, and that this process is similar to recalling previous situations or imagining potential ones.

The novelist Joe Meno writes about how a book is

> a place where we, as adults, still have the chance to engage in active imagining, translating word to image, connecting those images to memories, dreams, and larger ideas. Television, film, even the stage play, have already

been imagined for us, but the book, in whatever form we choose to interact with it, forces us to complete it.[64]

Indeed what is fascinating is the power of words to affect us quickly and immediately. Certainly this can happen with images but words are powerful also. In Ray Bradbury's dystopian novel, *Fahrenheit 451* (1953), the fireman Montag, dispatched to burn the books at an old lady's house, finds a volume land in his hands: he 'had only an instant to read a line, but it blazed in his mind for the next minute as if stamped there with fiery steel. "Time has fallen asleep in the afternoon sunshine."'[65]

Daniel Kahneman gives the example of displaying the following two words alongside each other:

Bananas   Vomit

Reading these words gives you an unpleasant feeling almost immediately, and your brain starts to create associations. This might be a temporal or causal association, perhaps around eating bananas and feeling ill. You might have recoiled physically as well as emotionally. Your memory has altered so that you are now highly receptive to recognize and respond to objects and concepts associated with vomit or bananas. Kahneman says you did not will this set of responses and you could not stop it: this is an example of how you think with your body, not just your brain:

> An idea that has been activated does not merely evoke one other idea. It activates many ideas, which in turn activate others. Furthermore, only a few of the activated ideas will register in consciousness; most of the work of associative thinking is silent, hidden from our conscious selves.[66]

If just two words can have this effect, then it is not surprising that we can be altered by reading a full-length book. Our brains also tend to impose a narrative on what we are reading, as evidenced by another brain experiment, involving reading proverbs with the error introduced of a word repeated. Participants were shown, for example:

A bird in the
the hand is worth
two in the bush

Two participants showed a marked improvement in spotting an error after low-level stimulation was applied to their brains to inhibit activity in the left hemisphere. It is suggested that this restriction of the left brain diminished pattern recognition, and enabled the subjects to develop, albeit briefly, a more literal-minded approach to reading.[67]

Privacy

An additional advantage of ereaders is an element of privacy. If the books we read make a statement about ourselves, from those on show in our homes to the book we are reading whilst commuting, then there is a display element to our reading habits. For books which are deemed literary or important, or are creating a buzz, we want others to know we are reading them:

> People have the mistaken notion that the thing you do with books is read them. Wrong ... People buy books for what the purchase says about them — their taste, their cultivation, their trendiness. Their aim ... is to connect themselves, or those to whom they give the books as gifts, with all the other refined owners.[68]

Consumption of books therefore is part of the development of our own identity, and we use books to say something about ourselves and to create our life space. Yet some readers may prefer others not to know what they are reading or purchasing. A study of middle school children in Texas discovered that ereaders could have the benefit of helping readers struggling with their reading.[69] Low-level readers were less keen for their peers to know which texts they were reading, and teachers could assign in a confidential way texts suitable for those who were struggling. The study also found that boys valued reading more on an ereader, perhaps because they could be seen to be using a gadget. The attitudes of girls to reading did not seem to be affected. There has been considerable research into gender differences around reading amongst children, with one UK study finding that girls enjoy reading more, hold more positive attitudes towards reading, and seek out more reading opportunities.[70] Overall girls are more engaged with reading, and this carries on into later life, with more women than men reading fiction, for example. Can the use of technology get more boys interested in reading, and break down the stereotype expressed by one secondary school boy in 2012: 'They're turning me into a geek. They're making us read books'?[71]

If digital reading can help to break down some of the anxieties about reading, it should help to broaden the base of readers. Generating much publicity in the media has been the sales growth in particular genres, such as romance and erotic fiction. The rise of what has been described as 'mummy porn' has been put down to the use of ereaders, on which nobody knows what you are reading. Sales of erotic novels have soared because, as one publisher said, 'You could be a mom, sitting in the park on a play day with the moms down the block and you could be reading a real kinky novel and nobody knows.'[72] Similarly some romance readers felt embarrassed buying this kind of fiction in a shop — the perfect solution is to download an ebook.

Reading apace

What does the brain research mean for the evolution of the book? There appear to be limits to how fast we can read, simply because of the limitations of the fovea.

But it is possible to imagine an ebook which simply reveals a few words at a time, at a set point on the page. We could then read without having to shift our gaze on the page, and up our reading speed by about three or four times. It is difficult to mimic this in present ebooks, since minimizing the words on the page simply results in larger and less focused type, and many readers would feel uncomfortable with so few words displayed.

But is the aim to speed up reading? Should not our habits learnt on the web, when we skim read and flit from one site to another, be discouraged when it comes to reading books? There is the potential to create a vast array of hyperlinks in books, whether to relevant websites, images, videos, or definitions. But when we reach this point, what is the difference between a book and a website? It is already possible to scroll through some ebooks rather than turn the pages, and this can be facilitated by eye-scrolling technology which recognizes when you reach the bottom of the screen. The Google generation of online users are expert at moving at a fast and furious pace in the search for information. Research into the behaviour of students and academics has revealed that 'users are not reading online in the traditional sense, indeed there are signs that new forms of "reading" are emerging as users "power browse" horizontally through titles, contents pages and abstracts going for quick wins. It almost seems that they go online to avoid reading in the traditional sense.'[73]

Should not books be helping us to slow down our thoughts and become more contemplative? It may depend on the type of book – sometimes you feel you simply have to race to the end of a book, to find out the denouement; other times you want the book to last forever. For example, *Cold Mountain* by Charles Frazier, with its slow pace and long descriptions, is a novel to be savoured and not rushed.

Kevin Kelly says that while books are good at developing a contemplative mind, screens encourage more utilitarian thinking:

> A new idea or unfamiliar fact will provoke a reflex to do something: to research the term, to query your screen 'friends' for their opinions, to find alternative views, to create a bookmark, to interact with or tweet the thing rather than simply contemplate it. Book reading strengthened our analytical skills, encouraging us to pursue an observation all the way down to the footnote. Screen reading encourages rapid pattern-making, associating this idea with another, equipping us to deal with the thousands of new thoughts expressed every day. The screen rewards, and nurtures, thinking in real time. We review a movie while we watch it, we come up with an obscure fact in the middle of an argument, we read the owner's manual of a gadget we spy in a store before we purchase it rather than after we get home and discover that it can't do what we need it to do.[74]

In order to lower our stress levels, we should sometimes slow down our reading and consequently our thinking, with benefits for our overall well-being. Richard Restak advocates training yourself to read at a much slower pace:

> Despite what you've heard from speed-reading advocates, that technique is only satisfactory when rapidly skimming newspapers or magazines for general information. In those instances, you care more about information and meaning than the words and style employed by the writer. ... Accustom yourself to reading at a slower rate and you'll gradually notice a sense of relaxation.[75]

We might also cultivate stronger social and family relationships, if we can switch off from our always-on, online personas. Sherry Turkle points out the dangers for our emotional lives of our obsession with emails and texts, to the detriment of even our close relationships. She gives the example of a high school child whose father used to 'read for pleasure and didn't mind being interrupted', but when books were replaced by the BlackBerry, it took effort to attract his attention and bring him out of that zone.[76]

What our time online might be doing to our brains is the subject of a piece by Nicholas Carr. In 'Is Google making us stupid?', he cites a regular online user: 'His thinking ... has taken on a "staccato" quality, reflecting the way he quickly scans short passages of text from many sources online. "I can't read War and Peace anymore", he admitted. "I've lost the ability to do that. Even a blog post of more than three or four paragraphs is too much to absorb. I skim it."'[77]

Also concerned about the impact of digital reading is the cognitive neuroscientist Maryanne Wolf. Will the glut of digital information to which we have access mean that readers do not have the time or the motivation to think through to a deeper level about what they are reading? 'Sound bites, text bites, and mind bites are a reflection of a culture that has forgotten or become too distracted by and too drawn to the next piece of new information to allow itself time to think.'[78] Effortless access to information through the portal of Google is not the same as developing the capacity to think for yourself; nor is watching a film the same as immersion in a novel where you imagine another world and enter the consciousness of the characters.

Reading the future

Reading as an activity is carrying on around us, from browsing news websites and scanning social networking sites, to reading text messages. We are still reading and literacy is regarded as a benefit to both individuals and the future success of our economies. Clearly identifiable is a link between literacy and life chances, including continuing in education, employability, and earnings.[79]

As Umberto Eco says, 'The Internet has returned us to the alphabet. If we thought we had become a purely visual civilisation, the computer returns us to Gutenberg's galaxy; from now on, everyone has to read.'[80] If we are looking to access information quickly, then the internet provides ready and mostly reliable answers. There is no longer the need to reach for a print encyclopedia. An argument with friends in the pub over the answer to a particular query, now comes to a quick end after consultation of a smartphone. User-generated and 'good enough' content on the web have replaced many reference titles. Mike Shatzkin comments on some categories of books, for example cookery and travel: 'What used to be delivered in books is now delivered more effectively in granular form on the internet.'[81]

Reading books on-screen is now a pleasant experience or perfectly functional depending on the device used. The evidence so far is that ereaders are most suited to straightforward linear reading of commercial fiction, and this is the way the market has moved.[82] There is more research to be carried out around our mental mapping of ebooks as compared to printed books. With the printed book, we are conscious of its length, how far through the text we have reached, and can visualize where in a novel a character first appeared. Losing this mental map may not matter at all, and a new generation may be happy to use hyperlinks and search tools to jump around a text. But does this mental map reveal something about the importance of reading in a linear fashion? A text with hyperlinks can be created with many routes through a book, and lots of links to outside resources, but perhaps our brains don't work that way? As Davida Charney argues, 'the development of linear text forms, with their careful sequencing of ideas, may not reflect constraints of the print medium so much as the needs of readers and writers who depend on the text to help them sequence the flow of ideas.'[83]

If books in digital form enable us to read faster, this may not necessarily be a good thing. To relax, to engage in deep thought are not encouraged by rushing through at speed. Just as we have a movement for slow food – in reaction to fast food – we should be advocating slow books – read aloud to children, broadcast on the radio, or taken at a leisurely pace in whatever format.

The research on the range and scale of book readership is difficult to assess, but we can draw some conclusions. There is no given that reading books has to be in terminal decline, even if it has suffered through competition from other media. Whereas once it was television which had a big impact on our leisure time, it is now the internet which is in turn having an impact on our media habits – yet some avid users of the internet still seem drawn to books. We can see the development of a reading class in many countries, who are still keen on books, but alongside a range of other media. Cultural differences abound and, for example, there is not yet the concept of the beach read in China, as Fangzhou Yang of Dook Publishing observes: 'There is now growing interest in taking a vacation among the middle class, but people tour around, going sightseeing and shopping, instead of lying on the beach to relax and read.'[84]

Why does reading of books remain important at all? The research into IQ suggests that it is the world of work which contributes most to the development of our vocabulary, rather than reading for pleasure. But other studies draw a link between reading for pleasure and reading effectively. The 2009 PISA report into reading and mathematics skills, which compared performance internationally among 15-year-olds in 65 countries, concluded:

46 Slow books

> Students who enjoy reading, and therefore make it a regular part of their lives, are able to build their reading skills through practice. PISA shows strong associations between reading enjoyment and performance. This does not mean that results show that enjoyment of reading has a direct impact on reading scores; rather, the finding is consistent with research showing that such enjoyment is an important precondition for becoming an effective reader.[85]

The National Endowment of Arts, in their research, found that readers of literature are more likely than non-literary readers to perform volunteer and charity work, visit art museums, attend performing arts events, and attend sporting events.[86]

Beyond any utilitarian approach to the importance of reading, we can go further to say that we have a need to tell and listen to stories:

> Both the artistic and scientific enterprises are the product of our need to reduce dimension and inflict some order on things. Think of the world around you, laden with trillions of details. Try to describe it and you will find yourself tempted to weave a thread into what you are saying. A novel, a story, a myth, or a tale, all have the same function: they spare us from the complexity of the world and shield us from its randomness.[87]

In the end, as Ian McEwan says about fiction: 'We have a hunger for talking and thinking about others and I don't think any other form can deliver that insider-ish feeling.'[88]

Notes

1 Interviewed by John Wilson on *Front Row*, BBC R4 programme, 7 December 2012.
2 Wim Knulst and Andries van den Broek, 'The Readership of Books in a Time of De-Reading', *Poetics* 31 (2003), pages 213–33; Wim Knulst and Gerbert Kraaykamp, 'Trends in Leisure Reading', *Poetics* 26 (1998), pages 21–41.
3 John P. Robinson and Geoffey Godbey, *Time for Life: The surprising ways Americans use their time*, Pennsylvania State University Press, 1999, page 150.
4 Linda M. Scott, 'Markets and Audiences', Chapter 4 of *The Enduring Book: Print culture in postwar America*, edited by David Paul Nord, Joan Shelley Rubin, and Michael Schudson, University of North Carolina Press, 2009, page 76.
5 National Endowment for the Arts, *Reading at Risk: A survey of literary reading in America*, Research Division Report No. 46, June 2004.
6 National Endowment for the Arts, *Reading on the Rise: A new chapter in American literacy*, Office of Research and Analysis, January 2009.
7 Jackie Huang of Andrew Nurnberg Associates, Beijing. Interviewed by the author, 15 January 2013.
8 Dale Southerton, Alan Warde, Shu-Li Cheng, and Wendy Olsen, 'Trajectories of Time Spent Reading as a Primary Activity: A comparison of the Netherlands, Norway, France, UK and USA', Centre for Research on Socio-Cultural Change, Working Paper No. 39, November 2007.
9 Ibid., page 24.
10 Ibid.

11 Kevin Kelly, 'Reading in a Whole New Way', *Smithsonian*, August 2010. Available at http://www.smithsonianmag.com/specialsections/40th-anniversary/Reading-in-a-Whole-New-Way.html#ixzz1xrBS4vic, accessed 23 September 2013.

12 Office for National Statistics, *General Lifestyle Survey Overview – a Report on the 2011 General Lifestyle Survey*, 7 March 2012, chapter 4.

13 Roger E. Bohn and James E. Short, *How Much Information? 2009 Report on American Consumers*, Global Information Industry Center, University of California, San Diego, December 2009.

14 Beverly Plester and Clare Wood, 'Exploring Relationships Between Traditional and New Media Literacies: British preteen texters at school', *Journal of Computer-Mediated Communication*, 14 (2009), page 1121.

15 James R. Flynn, *Are We getting Smarter? Rising IQ in the twenty-first century*, Cambridge University Press, 2012, loc 582 of 9750 in ebook.

16 Ibid., loc 1977 of 9750.

17 Ibid., loc 395 of 9750.

18 Eurobarometer Survey, *European Cultural Values*, September 2007. The fieldwork was carried out earlier that year.

19 Eurostat Pocketbook, *Cultural Statistics*, 2007.

20 Camilla Addey, *Readers and Non-Readers: A cross-cultural study in Italy and the UK*, Legas Publishing, 2008, page 28.

21 Ibid., page 44.

22 Annina Mousse, 'The Characteristics of the Finnish Book Publishing Business', research paper. Available at http://www.uta.fi/FAST/FIN/RESEARCH/mousse.pdf, accessed 23 September 2013.

23 OECD, *PISA 2009 Results: What Students Know and Can Do – Student Performance in Reading, Mathematics and Science* (Volume I), PISA, OECD Publishing, 2010.

24 Irmeli Halinen, Pirjo Sinko, and Reijo Laukkanen, 'A Land of Readers', *Educational Leadership*, 63:2 (2005), October, pages 72–75.

25 'Freedom of the Press 2011 – Finland'. Available at http://www.unhcr.org/refworld/docid/4e70938928.html, accessed 20 May 2013.

26 Research by the National Book Centre of Greece, http://www.ekebi.gr

27 Christina Banou and Angus Phillips, 'The Greek Publishing Industry and Professional Development', *Publishing Research Quarterly*, 24 (2008), pages 98–110.

28 Eurostat Pocketbook, *Cultural Statistics*, 2011.

29 OECD, *Let's Read Them a Story! The Parent Factor in Education*, PISA, OECD Publishing, 2012. Available at http://dx.doi.org/10.1787/9789264176232-en, accessed 23 September 2013.

30 Vanessa Martin, Catherine Bunting, and Anni Oskala, *Arts Engagement in England 2008/09: Findings from the taking part survey*, Arts Council, February 2010.

31 Pierre Bourdieu, *Distinction*, translated by Richard Nice, Routledge, 2010, page xxiv.

32 Wendy Griswold, *Regionalism and the Reading Class*, University of Chicago Press, 2008, page 67.

33 Shaoguang Wang, Deborah Davis, and Yanjie Bian, 'The Uneven Distribution of Cultural Capital: Book reading in urban China', *Modern China*, 32:3 (2006), page 332.

34 Information from Cheng Sanguo, CEO of bookdao.com, interviewed by the author, 15 January 2013.

35 O Instituto Paulo Montenegro e a ONG Ação Educativa, *INAF Brasil: O Indicador de Alfabetismo Funcional*, 2011.

36 Interviewed by the author, 20 March 2013.

37 Laura Miller, 'Perpetual Turmoil: Book retailing in the 21st century United States', *Logos*, 22:3 (2011), page 20.

38 Ofcom, Communications Market Report: UK, Research Document, 4 August 2011.

39 Ibid.

48 Slow books

40 Thomas Kilian, Nadine Hennigs, and Sascha Langner, 'Do Millennials read books or blogs? Introducing a media usage typology of the internet generation', *Journal of Consumer Marketing*, 29: 2 (2012).

41 Graeme McMillan, 'Viewers are Flocking to Streaming Video Content – and so are Advertisers', *Wired*, 3 January 2013.

42 Graeme Hutton and Maggie Fosdick, 'The Globalization of Social Media: Consumer relationships with brands evolve in the digital space', *Journal of Advertising Research* (2011), December, page 568.

43 Entertainment Software Association, *Essential Facts about the Computer and Video Game Industry*, 2011. Available from www.theESA.com

44 Figures for internet usage in the USA, from Nielsen NetView – June 2009 to June 2010.

45 Dennis Baron, *A Better Pencil: Readers, writers, and the digital revolution*, Oxford University Press, 2009, page 181.

46 Interviewed by the author, 19 November 2012.

47 Pew Research Centre, *The Rise of E-Reading*, report published 5 April 2012. Available at http://libraries.pewinternet.org/2012/04/04/the-rise-of-e-reading/, accessed 23 September 2013.

48 Interviewed by the author, 15 January 2013.

49 See Angus Phillips, 'Does the Book Have a Future?', in Simon Eliot and Jonathan Rose (eds), *A Companion to the History of the Book*, Blackwell, 2007.

50 Anne Mangen, 'Hypertext Fiction Reading: Haptics and immersion', *Journal of Research in Reading*, 31:4 (2008), page 408.

51 'The E-Reader Pilot at Princeton', Fall Semester 2009, page 14. Project web page: www.princeton.edu/ereaderpilot, accessed 20 May 2013.

52 Ibid., page 12.

53 M. Cristina Pattuelli and Debbie Rabina, 'Forms, effects, function: LIS students' attitudes towards portable e-book readers', *Aslib Proceedings*, 62:3 (2010), pages 228–44.

54 Ibid., pages 235 and 240.

55 Jan M. Noyesa and Kate J. Garland, 'Computer-vs. paper-based tasks: Are they equivalent?', *Ergonomics*, 51:9 (2008), pages 1352–75.

56 Johannes Gutenberg University, Media Convergence Research Unit, 'Different reading devices, different modes of reading?', October 2011. The full findings were published in F. Kretzschmar, D. Pleimling, J. Hosemann, S. Füssel, I. Bornkessel-Schlesewsky, et al., 'Subjective Impressions Do Not Mirror Online Reading Effort: Concurrent EEG-eye-tracking evidence from the reading of books and digital media', *PLoS ONE*, 8:2 (2013).

57 The early results of this study, led by Daniel Roth, MD, an associate clinical professor at Robert Wood Johnson School of Medicine, were presented at the 116th Annual Meeting of the American Academy of Ophthalmology. Available at http://www.aao.org/newsroom/release/20121111b.cfm, accessed 28 December 2012.

58 Stanislas Dehaene, *Reading in the Brain: The new science of how we read*, Penguin, 2009.

59 Ibid., page 2.

60 Stanislas Dehaene and Laurent Cohen, 'The unique role of the visual word form area in reading', *Trends in Cognitive Sciences*, 15:6 (2011), page 254.

61 A. Castro-Caldas, K. M. Petersson, A. Reis, S. Stone-Elander, and M. Ingvar, 'The Illiterate Brain: Learning to read and write during childhood influences the functional organization of the adult brain', *Brain*, 121 (1998).

62 Interviewed by the author, 29 March 2013. See also Corrie Goldman, 'This is your brain on Jane Austen, and Stanford researchers are taking notes'. Available at http://news.stanford.edu/news/2012/september/austen-reading-fmri-090712.html#sthash.lcK1peF5.dpuf, accessed 1 March 2013.

63 Nicole K. Speer, Jeremy R. Reynolds, Khena M. Swallow, and Jeffrey M. Zacks, 'Reading Stories Activates Neural Representations of Visual and Motor Experiences', *Psychological Science*, 20:8 (2009), pages 989–99.

64 Joe Meno, 'A Book is a Place', in Jeff Martin and C. Max Magee (eds), *The Late American Novel: Writers on the future of books*, Soft Skull Press, 2011, ebook, page 10.

65 Ray Bradbury, *Fahrenheit 451*, HarperVoyager, 2012 ebook edition, 22 per cent. The quotation comes from Alexander Smith's *Dreamthorp: A book of essays written in the country*, first published in 1863.

66 Daniel Kahneman, *Thinking, Fast and Slow*, Penguin, 2011, page 52.

67 Allan W. Snyder, Elaine Mulcahy, Janet L. Taylor, D. John Mitchell, Perminder Sachdev, and Simon C. Gandevia, 'Savant-Like Skills Exposed in Normal People by Suppressing the Left Fronto-Temporal Lobe', *Journal of Integrative Neuroscience*, 2:2 (2003).

68 Leonard Riggio, quoted in Philip Kotler and Gary Armstrong, *Principles of Marketing*, 9th edition, *Financial Times* / Prentice Hall (2001), page 183.

69 Miranda Twyla, Dara Williams-Rossi, Kary A. Johnson, and Nancy McKenzie, 'Reluctant Readers in Middle School: Successful engagement with text using the e-reader', *International Journal of Applied Science and Technology*, 1:6 (2011), November.

70 Christina Clark, with David Burke, *Boys' Reading Commission: A review of existing research to underpin the Commission*, National Literacy Trust, 2012.

71 Overheard by the author, Oxford, 2012.

72 Brenda Knight, associate publisher of Cleis Press, quoted in '"Kinky" ebooks sell fast in age of digital privacy', *Daily Telegraph*, 21 May 2012.

73 Ian Rowlands, David Nicholas, Peter Williams, Paul Huntington, Maggie Fieldhouse, Barrie Gunter, Richard Withey, Hamid R. Jamali, Tom Dobrowolski, Carol Tenopir, 'The Google Generation: The information behaviour of the researcher of the future', *Aslib Proceedings*, 60:4 (2008), page 295.

74 Kevin Kelly, 'Reading in a Whole New Way', *Smithsonian*, August 2010. Available at http://www.smithsonianmag.com/specialsections/40th-anniversary/Reading-in-a-Whole-New-Way.html#ixzz1xrBS4vic, accessed 23 September 2013.

75 Richard Restak, *Mozart's Brain and the Fighter Pilot: Unleashing your brain's potential*, Three Rivers Press, 2001, pages 125–6.

76 Sherry Turkle, *Alone Together: Why we expect more from technology and less from each other*, Basic Books, 2011, page 268.

77 Nicholas Carr, 'Is Google Making Us Stupid?', *The Atlantic*, July/August 2008.

78 Maryanne Wolf, 'Our "Deep Reading" Brain: Its digital evolution poses questions', Nieman Reports, Summer 2010. Available at http://www.nieman.harvard.edu/reports/article/102396/Our-Deep-Reading-Brain-Its-Digital-Evolution–Poses-Questions.aspx, accessed 23 September 2013.

79 See, for example, S. Grenier, S. Jones, J. Strucker, T. S. Murray, G. Gervais and S. Brink, *Learning Literacy in Canada: Evidence from the International Survey of Reading Skills*, Statistics Canada, 2008.

80 Jean-Claude Carrière and Umberto Eco, *This Is Not the End of the Book*, Harvill Secker, 2011, page 4.

81 Interviewed by the author, 13 March 2013.

82 In his book *Burning the Page*, Jason Merkoski, a member of the launch team at Amazon, says that the Kindle was 'targeted at readers buying genre fiction like romance books and sci-fi and bestsellers. Even in print, these books aren't stylistically nuanced' (Sourcebooks, 2013, loc 663 of 3546 in ebook). In the UK market in 2012, fiction sales took 65 per cent of the ebook market by volume; and 27 per cent of volume sales in fiction were in ebook form. Lisa Campbell, 'Fiction Rules 2012 E-book Sales', *The Bookseller*, 4 April 2013.

83 Davida Charney, 'The Impact of Hypertext on Processes of Reading and Writing', in Susan J. Hilligoss and Cynthia L. Selfe (eds), *Literacy and Computers*, Modern Language Association (2004), pages 238–63.

84 Interviewed by the author, 8 February 2013.

85 OECD, *PISA 2009 at a Glance*, PISA, OECD Publishing, 2010, page 66. A 2013 study from the UK Institute of Education suggested that reading for enjoyment directly

50 Slow books

influences performance at school, with children who read for pleasure, compared to those who read little, making more progress in mathematics, vocabulary, and spelling. Alice Sullivan and Matt Brown, 'Social inequalities in cognitive scores at age 16: The role of reading', CLS Working Paper, 10 (2013).

86 National Endowment for the Arts, *Reading at Risk*, op. cit.

87 Nassim Nicholas Taleb, *The Black Swan: The impact of the highly improbable*, Penguin, 2007, loc 1674 of 8278 in ebook.

88 Interviewed by Rachel Cooke in the *Observer*, 19 August 2012. A 2013 study showed that reading literary fiction aids empathy, social perception and emotional intelligence. David Comer Kidd and Emanuele Castano, 'Reading Literary Fiction Improves Theory of Mind', *Science*, 342: 6156 (October 2013), Pages 377–80.

3

CONDEMNED TO BE FREE? CONTENT IN A DIGITAL WORLD

The third key driver, along with authorship and readership, underpinning the book industry is the system of copyright. This provides an economic incentive for authors to write, and for publishers to invest in the production and marketing of books. Without the protection of copyright, and its enforcement, there would be widespread pirating and plagiarism of books and their contents, with little reward feeding back to the copyright owners or licensees.

Copyright in its present form faces significant challenges, not just from piracy but also from the expectations of users, many of whom regard it as acceptable to download content for free – this includes music and films. In order to highlight what is happening to books, this chapter examines the experience of other media industries, as well as legitimate challenges to the present system of copyright, which attempt to update the regime in the light of a digitally connected world.

The system of copyright

The year 2010 saw the three hundredth anniversary of the Statute of Anne, which is recognized as the first initiative in the world to give rights to copyright holders to prevent copying by unauthorized third parties. Vested firstly in the author, the right to control copying could be licensed to a bookseller or publisher. The system in place in the twenty-first century gives the initial right to the author of a work, and the copyright line on the back of a book's title page serves to confirm this. The author is then able to publish the work themselves, or to license a publisher to issue the work. Usually the author will retain the copyright under the terms of the licence.

The term of copyright in the USA and Europe is 70 years from the end of the year of the author's death, providing an economic benefit during their lifetime and for their heirs. The right to control copying by others, usually exercised by the

52 Content in a digital world

publisher, means that income is derived from direct sales of a book or from giving others the right to copy – for example selling serial rights to a newspaper, or licensing the translation rights to another publisher. Legal proceedings can be taken out against those who breach the terms of copyright, giving teeth to the regime.

The tension in the copyright system is that it has to balance access to content against the rights of the creator.

> On the one hand, copyright aims to promote public disclosure and dissemination of works of 'authorship'; on the other hand, it seeks to confer on the creators the power to restrict or deny distribution of their works. This conflict is reflected in the tension between public benefit and private reward inscribed in the full title of ... the Statute of Anne ... *An Act for the Encouragement of Learning, by Vesting the Copies of Printed Books in the Authors or Purchasers of such Copies during the Times therein mentioned.*[1]

This tension is eased by creating a distinction between the idea of a work and its expression. Ideas cannot be copyrighted and are therefore free to all; the *expression* of the idea in whatever form is protected. The system also derives from the traditional idea of authorship, and the notion of artistic genius, with reward being given to imagination rather than simply application. Copyrighted works have to pass a test of originality, and the tendency is for authorship to rest with the person who originated the work rather than some later collaborator. For example extensive editorial work on a novel would not allow another person to claim co-authorship. Given that digital channels of publication allow considerable opportunities for collaboration and the creation of what may be considered derivative works, how should these issues be handled?

There are philosophical objections to the system of copyright, which originate from different quarters. Firstly some authors simply want to be read by as many people as possible, and do not wish to see barriers erected by copyright as a deterrent. Some content creators make their living by other means, and are happy to see their work widely viewed and passed around. Take the example of a photographer who posts their work on the web and is then happy for others to view it for free – they may well be delighted to see their image reused. One reservation might be that the creator should be duly acknowledged in any further reuse; another would concern the possibility that a commercial company could profit from the reuse.

A powerful advocate of fewer controls on content is Lawrence Lessig, who argues that a free culture should support and protect creators and innovators. 'It does this directly by granting intellectual property rights. But it does so indirectly by limiting the reach of those rights, to guarantee that follow-on creators and innovators remain as free as possible from the control of the past.'[2] He regards a free culture as increasingly the casualty in the war on piracy, and thinks that the property right of copyright is no longer a balanced right. 'The opportunity to create and transform becomes weakened in a world in which creation requires permission and creativity must check with a lawyer.'[3]

Content in a digital world **53**

One artist who some may regard as merely derivative is John Stezaker, who won the 2012 Deutsche Borse prize for photography. His images are created by cutting up the work of other photographers, from film stills, postcards, and magazines, and producing collages. Early in his career he was shunned by some photographers, who believed he was defacing the work of others. The jury of the prize, however, recognized Stezaker's achievement in exploring 'the subversive force of the found image'.[4]

An exercise to legitimize a more open approach to the use of content is the Creative Commons movement – a founding member was Lessig – which has devised a licence through which authors and other creators can allow their work to be copied with due acknowledgement. They might well also stipulate that no work should be reused for commercial gain, which would stop a commercial publisher picking up on a work and making it publicly available for profit.

For example, on Flickr, users can choose from a variety of licences to apply to their work. *Attribution* means that others are allowed to copy, distribute, display, and perform your copyrighted work – and derivative works based upon it – but only if they give you credit. *Share Alike* means that others are allowed to distribute derivative works but only under a licence which is identical to the licence of your work. The book *Art Space Tokyo* (2010), by Ashley Rawlings and Craig Mod, is licensed under a Creative Commons licence. The copyright page carries this message:

> Normally, this space is a cue for a publisher to get stuffy. Don't copy this, only use a small portion of that. How about: copy the hell out of this thing. Scan your favourite maps and give them to your friends. Shoot them out of a blimp. E-mail interviews to family members. Post them on your blog. You can do anything – anything – with the text in this book as long as it's not commercial and you provide attribution.[5]

Such licences allow room for the creative mixing of the work of different originators – and for the full use of the possibilities afforded by digital media. A remix work might overlay text on images. A popular example was the picture of US Secretary State Hilary Clinton on a military plane wearing a pair of sunglasses. In the picture placed before, the previous incumbent of the office, Condoleezza Rice, is saying to George Bush, 'So then I sent her a text saying I think I left my favourite sunglasses in the desk'; Clinton texts back 'Sorry Condi, haven't seen them'. If successful, such images can become memes which spread around social media and the internet.

Others go further and believe that content should be free and freely available now that it is available in a digital form. There is a reason to pay for a physical book which has been printed and shipped, but not for an ebook which bears no equivalent cost. In fact the marginal cost of an ebook – the extra cost of producing one additional unit – is virtually zero. We can source this idea back to Stewart Brand, who in 1985 commented about the digital age:

54 Content in a digital world

> There's a couple of interesting paradoxes that we are working here. …
> On the one hand information wants to be expensive, because it's so valuable.
> The right information in the right place just changes your life. On the other
> hand, information wants to be free, because the cost of getting it out is get-
> ting lower and lower all the time. So you have these two fighting against
> each other.[6]

There is no doubt that an underlying philosophy of the web is that there should be
no charge to access content, and this is the idealism behind Wikipedia and open
source software such as Linux. Of course there are economic benefits from free
content for some players, such as Google, who rely on a plentiful source around
which to build their services. Kevin Kelly, the co-founder of *Wired* magazine,
believes that as the value of digital content is zero, creators must find other ways of
sourcing an income:

> As copies have been dethroned, the economic model built on them is col-
> lapsing. In a regime of superabundant free copies, copies lose value. They are
> no longer the basis of wealth. Now relationships, links, connection and
> sharing are. Value has shifted away from a copy toward the many ways to
> recall, annotate, personalize, edit, authenticate, display, mark, transfer and engage
> a work. Authors and artists can make (and have made) their livings selling
> aspects of their works other than inexpensive copies of them. They can sell
> performances, access to the creator, personalization, add-on information, the
> scarcity of attention (via ads), sponsorship, periodic subscriptions – in short,
> all the many values that cannot be copied.[7]

In opposition to these views are the concerns that without any direct charge for
content, the content producers will in the end go out of business. There would be
no reason to invest in projects if there is no anticipated and predictable return. This
would apply to authors and their investment of time, and to publishers who sign
up new authors and invest in editing, marketing, and distributing their works.

A further protection for authors is the system of moral rights, which derives from
the *droit moral* in France. Although open to interpretation country by country, two
basic rights are generally recognized: the right to paternity, which ensures that an
author's name is attached to their work; and the right to integrity, which prevents
an author's work being distorted by, for example, editorial interventions. As Mira
T. Sundara Rajan suggests, 'The purpose of moral rights is to protect the author
from suffering the consequences of moral, intellectual, or spiritual harm inflicted on
him through the mistreatment of his work.'[8] A judgement in the French courts
revealed interesting dimensions to moral rights, in a country where they are often
seen as more important than economic rights. A descendant of Victor Hugo
(1802–85) had gone to court to try and prevent the publication of sequels to *Les
Misérables*. The notion was upheld that in the jurisdiction of France, there is no
limit to the period for which moral rights can be asserted, but after a prolonged

legal battle, the ruling in 2007 went in favour of the publishers. The court decided that the new books did not violate the author's right of integrity, despite evidence that Hugo himself disliked the idea of a sequel. This has implications for fan fiction, which is already broadly allowed if non-commercial (and therefore does not attract sanction for breaching the author's copyright), but now it appears that if such works do not alter the author's original, they do not violate the author's moral right of integrity.[9]

Music industry

There are varying viewpoints as to the usefulness of the comparison, but parallels with the music industry are often made. An industry which first resisted down-loading and then found it had to embrace it, has suffered a significant decline in the face of the switch to digital away from physical products. Alongside a small revival in sales of vinyl, CD sales have fallen consistently and have not been replaced in revenue terms by the income from legitimate downloads through such mechanisms as iTunes.

Although they may not publicly admit it, many are happy to pass music around their friends and family, and pay nothing for music from downloading sites. As the streaming of movies becomes more popular, with greater bandwidth available, it is also becoming more common to download films for free. The widely held view is that where the music industry went wrong was to resist the downloading of music and to take on file-sharing sites such as Napster. If legal methods of downloading had been easy to use, and promoted from the beginning, perhaps the culture of consumers would have adapted to a digital environment without heading off in a different direction? This is seen as a key lesson for the book industry.

There have been interesting studies of what has happened in the music industry. In the UK, there was a precipitous drop in sales of music with the advent of digitization: sales dropped by around a third in only seven years, from total revenues of £1.2bn in 2004 to £800m in 2011. The revenues from digital music reached £282m in 2011 (a growth of 25 per cent on the previous year) but clearly digital sales had still not made up for the fall in sales of the physical. Examining unit sales, CD sales had dropped by nearly a half since 2004: 86.2m units in 2011, compared with 163.4m in 2004; whilst vinyl only represented 0.3 per cent of the overall sales.[10]

Although the USA saw a small increase in album sales in 2011 (1.4 per cent), overall sales had fallen every year since 2004. The unit sales of CDs had dropped by two-thirds since 2004, to 224m, and revenue from recorded music fell 52 per cent from 2000 to 2010. The year 2011 saw digital downloads take half of the overall market (by unit) for the first time.[11]

There is no doubt that in some countries the culture of downloading music for free has taken hold. Despite legal action being taken against sites such as Pirate Bay, there is little sign of the enforcement being successful in its overall impact. A 2012 report highlighted the top five countries for illegal downloads as the USA, UK,

Italy, Canada, and Brazil.[12] As one method of access is closed down, others become more popular, for example using converters to create MP3 files from YouTube videos.

Meanwhile in France, a tough stance against illegal downloads appeared to have brought about an increase in sales, as reported early in 2012:

> More than two years after France approved a tough crackdown on copyright cheats, the agency that oversees it sent its first cases to the courts last week. Some repeat offenders may temporarily be cut off from the Internet. Studies show that the appeal of piracy has waned in France since the so-called three-strikes law, hailed by the music and movie industries and hated by advocates of an open Internet, went into effect. Digital sales, which were slow to get started in France, are growing. Music industry revenues are starting to stabilize. 'I think more and more French people understand that artists should get paid for their work,' said Pascal Nègre, president of Universal Music France. 'I think everybody has a friend who has received an e-mail. This creates a buzz. There is an educational effect.'[13]

Sweden is another country where the evidence suggests that a tougher stance has had an effect on piracy. A law introduced in 2009 made the chances of being prosecuted much more likely, and this had an immediate impact on overall internet traffic, which reduced overnight by 40 per cent. A study carried out by Adrian Adermon and Che-Yuan Liang suggested that pirated music appeared to be a strong substitute for legal music: for each per cent reduction in piracy brought about as a result of the new law, there were significant sales increases for music in both physical and digital form (0.72 and 1.31 per cent respectively). They found a weaker connection in the area of movie sales. The authors doubted the effectiveness of such controls in the longer run, however, as they found the effects of the law weakened after only six months.[14]

A study of music collections in the USA and Germany showed that around half of the digital files possessed by 18–29-year-olds derived from either free downloads or copies from friends and family. Copying from friends and family was comparable in scale and prevalence to downloading for free. The extent of this kind of copying is only likely to increase as the authorities take action against download sites.[15]

As can be seen, the effect of free downloading has been to take value out of the music industry, and a culture has taken hold amongst consumers where it is acceptable to share files. Some artists have also encouraged this culture, either through their public statements or through the issuing of free downloads. In June 2008, Joss Stone spoke out in favour of piracy and the sharing of music:

> I think it's great. I love it. I think it's brilliant, and I'll tell you why. Music should be shared. I believe that this is how music turned into, like, some crazy business. Now, the only part about music that I dislike is the business that is attached to it. Now, if music is free, then there is no business. There

is just music. So, I like it. I think that we should share it. It's OK. If one person buys it, it's totally cool. Burn it up. Share it with your friends. I don't care. I don't care how you hear it, as long as you hear it. As long as you come to my show and, like, have a great time and listen to the live show, it's totally cool.[16]

A successful artist such as Joss Stone can afford to be relaxed about illegal downloads, but she also puts her finger on the other route available to musicians to make an income – touring and live shows. Ageing bands who are seeing a decline in their royalty income always have the option of reforming and launching a live tour. There is not just the share of income from ticket sales but also from merchandise such as T-shirts and DVDs. As Patrik Wikström observes:

> The loss of revenue from recorded music is … able to explain the increase in the number of events. For obvious reasons, a live music experience is difficult to digitize, and is therefore considerably easier to control compared to those areas of the industry which have been affected more profoundly by digital technologies. Artists who previously were able to earn their livelihood from recorded music have greater and greater difficulties sustaining their businesses. As a consequence, more and more artists resort to touring, which has caused the number of yearly concert events to grow.[17]

Authors of books do take to the road to promote their latest work, and some are starting to charge for appearances at events and literary festivals, but the income stream is less certain than for successful musicians. Would any author fill a football stadium with over 50,000 people paying £60 a time? It is difficult to see how they can be relaxed about giving their works away for free. As we saw in the previous chapter, Paulo Coelho sees free downloads of his books as an effective form of marketing, but a culture of free downloads in which this is commonplace would have a substantial effect on book sales.

The market for music has been considerably depressed by the widespread use of free downloads. But does this matter, if the quantity and quality of music stay the same? Joel Waldfogel has attempted to use quantitative techniques to measure the quality of music in the period since the arrival of Napster.[18] He examined, for example, lists compiled by critics and music played on the radio, to see if there has been a decline in quality, and his view was that there continues to be a flow of new, high-quality material. This is in the face of sharp reductions in income for the music industry. His conclusion was that the costs of bringing music to market have also reduced, with lower costs for creation, promotion, and distribution.

In fact it is now very easy for an artist or band to record their own music and post it on the internet – do they really need the record industry? The phenomenal success of Lana Del Rey, who posted her single 'Video Games' on YouTube, shows what can be done. She first posted the home video in May 2010 and by the end of the year it had been viewed 20m times. The already established band

58 Content in a digital world

Radiohead went straight to their fans with the release of the album *In Rainbows* in 2007 on the internet. Deploying their 'honesty box' approach, they asked people to give what they wanted by way of a price for the download of the album. Having originally thought they were subverting the record labels, by 2013 Thom Yorke reflected they may simply have been playing into the hands of technology companies such as Apple and Google: 'They have to keep commodifying things to keep the share price up, but in doing so they have made all content, including music and newspapers, worthless, in order to make their billions.'[19]

Why record at all with a record label? Unofficial recordings, internet videos, and live shows will all spread word of mouth about an artist, and touring has the potential to provide a satisfactory income. Jeremy Denk, writing about recording by classical musicians, sums up some of the tensions which need to be resolved:

> Every year, classical musicians record themselves for posterity. The days when you could make money doing it are largely gone, but we persist. It's a way to be visible, to escape the fleetingness of performance, and to reach people who will never hear you in a concert. ... at lunch in midtown, my manager spoke to me sternly, paternally: 'We need something to talk about, to talk up, something for you to sell at your concerts.' And fatefully, business met vanity.[20]

So recordings offer a permanence, just as a book does. They can be heard in 50 years' time, discussed by critics and fans alike, and still offer a business model which just about works.

Newspapers

Another media industry which has seen the value sucked out of it is newspapers. In the USA, by 2009, the industry was selling 44m copies a day – fewer than at any time since the 1940s. In many countries the industry has fallen victim to a downward spiral, with falling revenues pushing up cover prices, which in turn force down circulation. Although online advertising has shown growth, this has not made up for the shortfall in print advertising. At the same time newspapers have to produce new kinds of content, from a social media presence to video. The paradox is that newspapers are read in ever greater numbers on the web and on mobile phones, where their content is mostly free. The publisher of the *Boston Globe*, Christopher Mayer, said in 2011: 'We have never had more consumers of our content. We have over 50 per cent penetration in this marketplace between print and digital.'[21]

The challenge for newspapers is to square the circle of a decline in revenues whilst competing effectively in a digital environment.

> The contemporary newsroom has fewer articles to produce after trims in the physical size of paper and reduction of the space devoted to news. But the remaining editors and reporters are also being stretched further by the need

to generate content suitable for smartphones and tablets as well as establishing a social media presence. This is all in addition to putting out the print paper daily and feeding breaking news to websites.[22]

The evidence suggests a decline in quality journalism as a result of lower income and thinner papers. In 2013 the *Columbia Journalism Review* examined over a ten-year period the number of long-form articles (over 2,000 words) published in a variety of up-market papers. Aside from *The New York Times*, where the numbers remained stable, papers such as the *Los Angeles Times* and the *Washington Post* saw steep drops. In 2003 the *Los Angeles Times* published 1,776 long-form articles, and in 2012 the figure was 256; in 2003 the *Washington Post* published 2,755 such articles, and in 2012 the figure was 1,378. True newspapers now publish picture galleries and videos as part of their coverage, but the figures show the turmoil within the industry over a decade.[23]

An article in *The Economist* back in 2006 considered the landscape of the newspaper industry, and judged that the gradual disappearance of the newspaper was a cause for concern, but not for panic. Newspapers were cutting back on journalism, trying out new business models (such as free newspapers), and we could see the early growth of citizen journalism. Today this includes videos taken on smartphones, for example during the Arab Spring of 2011, or bloggers writing about politics and breaking a political story. Overall their main concern was around the public role of the 4th Estate – would this continue? – and yet they found this was made more powerful with the growth of the internet:

> The usefulness of the press goes much wider than investigating abuses or even spreading general news; it lies in holding governments to account – trying them in the court of public opinion. The internet has expanded this court. Anyone looking for information has never been better equipped. People no longer have to trust a handful of national papers or, worse, their local city paper. News-aggregation sites such as Google News draw together sources from around the world. The website of Britain's *Guardian* now has nearly half as many readers in America as it does at home.[24]

Eventually, however, aggregation sites need to have content to pull together, and if newspapers spend less on journalism, the end-game will be news feeds all pulling in content from each other. Someone has to source, write, and edit the stories in the first place, beyond simply rewriting the press releases issued by organizations. The media guru Clay Shirky sees only one way ahead given the convergence of different media in front of consumers:

> The classic description of a commodity market uses milk. If you own the only cow for 50 miles, you can charge usurious rates, because no one can undercut you. If you own only one of a hundred such cows, though, then everyone can undercut you, so you can't charge such rates. In a competitive environment like that, milk becomes a commodity, something whose price is

60 Content in a digital world

set by the market as a whole. Owning a newspaper used to be like owning the only cow, especially for regional papers. Even in urban markets, there was enough segmentation – the business paper, the tabloid, the alternative weekly – and high enough costs to keep competition at bay. No longer. The internet commodifies the business of newspapers.[25]

By contrast to a book, a print newspaper is a throwaway item, easily discarded into the recycling. It looks as if its days are numbered as its readers get ever older. Readers have and are switching to online or mobile access, and a web article can be saved to access another day, forwarded on to a friend, or highlighted in a blog. It can be retrieved years later from the newspaper's archive. Since good, independent journalism should remain an essential part of our society, the challenge is to establish a secure way for it to be funded. At the moment it looks as though the answer has to be multiple revenue streams. Paywalls have been introduced with so-called metered access, where users have so many free views before being encouraged to take out a subscription (this approach seems to have worked for *The New York Times*), and charging for tablet editions, but while a range of content is free to view on the web, users will pursue this option. An interesting development does offer some respite for traditional media brands. With the growth in the use of mobile devices, more than a quarter of the US population now gets news in this way, and 'these mobile news consumers are even more likely to turn to news organizations directly, through apps and home pages, rather than search or recommendations – strengthening the bond with traditional brands'.[26]

Is the crisis in newspapers the same all over the world? The combination of lower sales and advertising revenues, with the growth in online news, is common in North America and Europe. In Spain, for example, the quality daily *El Pais* cut a third of its staff in 2012.[27] In Germany, in 2011, advertising revenue was 43 per cent lower than it had been in 2000.[28] By contrast in India, where the level of digital penetration is substantially lower, newspapers continue to thrive and as literacy levels rise, there are opportunities for growth:

> There are [in 2012] an estimated eighty thousand individual newspapers, eighty-five per cent of which are printed in one of India's twenty-two individual official regional languages, and the circulation of English-language newspapers is expanding by about one and a half per cent annually. Many non-English language newspapers are growing three times as fast, as about twenty million more Indians become literate each year. But, because English-language newspapers attract an up-scale readership, they draw seventy per cent of the available ad dollars.[29]

The lessons for the book

What can we learn from the experiences of both the music and newspaper industries?

From music we can learn that to some extent the genie is already out of the bottle. It is possible that some short-term gains can be made in the battle against piracy and illegal downloads, but severe controls are not likely to last long. Ian Hargreaves, in his 2011 UK report into intellectual property, concluded that we should not expect tougher enforcement alone to solve the problem of copyright infringement.[30] Industry experts believe that the best solution is to make it as easy as possible to download content in a legal manner. The service offered by, for example, Amazon for books is similar to that of iTunes for music and it is now very easy to download an ebook and start reading immediately. The question of ownership of music has entered a new phase, with some users happy to abandon their music collections (or never start them in the first place) in favour of streamed services such as Spotify. For a monthly fee, they have access to all the music they could ever want to listen to, and no clutter from CDs or LPs. By 2012 the music industry earned 20 per cent of its digital revenues from streaming services. The record labels have had a torrid time but have emerged leaner and stronger, and willing to offer the services artists want, including marketing and promotion.

On the face of it, books are different from music, because they cannot easily be broken down in the same way as albums. Mixing content from 30 different novels into your own playlist enables you to create your own William Burroughs title, but for most readers it would be deeply unsatisfying. However, for non-fiction works, part of the book may be all the reader wants, and breaking down works so that they can be sold by the chapter makes some sense. Those who suggest the book is merely a container are keen to see it broken up in the same way as an album, with chapters readily available. Yet the marginal cost argument still applies, whether the book is whole or subdivided – there is no extra cost to the new download of an ebook so the inexorable direction is towards free. Further, if content on the web is free, why should this not apply to books as well?

The passing of music around friends and family, which appears to be encouraged by efforts to control official piracy, does offer parallels for the book. The printed book is often passed on round the family unit or amongst friends, and consumers would like to do the same with an ebook. Controls using digital rights management (DRM) by and large prevent this happening, but can they last?

From newspapers we can see the growth of a global audience for content and we will return to this theme in chapter 5. Alongside the democratization of content, with so many different sources of news, and the reach of the internet, there is a trend towards commoditization. An elite readership may pay for content, but the majority will resist this move. The mass of free content on the internet calls into question the value of published information – is what is available on the internet 'good enough'? We can see an equivalent development in the area of travel publishing, where user-generated content is replacing the authority of printed travel guides. Travel publishing saw a consistent decline in sales from 2006 until 2012.[31] Alongside the effect on sales of the financial crisis during this period, there was also the growth of travel websites such as TripAdvisor, which posts user reviews and has developed a new business model around click-throughs and display advertising. In

62 Content in a digital world

the area of journalism we can see an emphasis on writers finding their own audience. For example, Forbes has a large team of contributors – bloggers, academics, and experts – who are paid according to the size of their audience. This encourages them to promote themselves through social media in order to increase their earnings.[32]

The means to buy a digital book are there and are quite straightforward. But if the expectation is that digital content should be inexpensive, if not free, the value of the industry of books will be reduced – just as has happened in the music industry. It is difficult to see that value being replaced by other means, whether live events, advertising, or merchandising.

When Chris Anderson wrote *Free* (2009), he put forward the thesis that low marginal costs enable companies to trade in new and creative ways. Why not offer items for free whilst making gains in other directions?[33] For example, free wi-fi in a coffee shop encourages custom. For non-fiction he saw parallels with music whereby free downloads would boost the author's speech-giving or consultancy career, just as downloads are good marketing for an artist's concerts. But he still saw the business model for a book in terms of a physical copy. Authors could be happy to give away free digital copies on the basis that the overall sales would expand of the physical book. With the growth in sales of ebooks, authors cannot afford to be so relaxed about a move towards free content.

We could update the idea of free and imagine a model in which the reader only pays once they have finished a book. They either choose to pay, as a satisfied reader, or have a free trial which expires once they have read the last chapter. This would, however, provide a significant disadvantage for an industry which relies on many books being bought and either not read or left unfinished.

Where should authors stand in what is sometimes a highly polarized debate? Intuitively perhaps they should come down in favour of open access to content, rather than pitch their tents with large media corporations. According to Mira T. Sundara Rajan:

> The position of authors makes them at once dependent on their publishers and antagonistic to them – at once for and against free access. Not surprisingly, many authors are sympathetic to the goals of open access movements, but the problem of economic survival – to say nothing of the desire for financial success – may align them with publishers.[34]

Her view of the Creative Commons model is that it is a solution for those who 'do not need, or do not want, to earn money for their creative work'.[35] Further, she sees it, despite its populist rhetoric, as still preoccupied with authorial control, for it offers considerable protection for the author in terms of attribution, as an author can choose the method by which they want to be attributed.

For most authors, the system of copyright still holds its attractions. On the 'what if' principle, just imagine your book does become a bestseller, you would want a system in place which enables you to benefit from those sales. Agreed, for most authors this is not going to happen, but there is comfort in having the arrangement there. The poet Wendy Cope has experienced at first hand the perils of free access to her work. Because her poems are short and very easy to post online, she was faced with the prospect that no one need ever buy her work. Indeed she came across many poems which had somehow become detached from their authorship, as a result of being posted online anonymously.

> My poems are all over the internet. I've managed to get them removed from one or two sites that were major offenders, but there are dozens, if not hundreds of sites displaying poems without permission. If I Google the title of one of my poems, it is almost always there somewhere, and I can download it and print it out. I'm sure that this must affect sales of my books.[36]

She feels that on her tombstone the words should be inscribed, *Wendy Cope. All rights reserved*. You can buy a mug inscribed with the title of one of her poems, 'Making Cocoa for Kingsley Amis', but it is doubtful that the income from these sales is sufficient compensation for the lost income.

Piracy

Although the processes leading up to a book's publication have been digital for a while, from the original author's file through typesetting and design work to the dispatch of the final file to the printer, the final product remained analogue for some time. The printed book has the benefit of making piracy more difficult, as pirated copies can be seized and destroyed. By contrast digital books are very easy to pirate, and no DRM system is immune to attack. Publishers, individually and collectively through trade associations, are engaged in a long-running battle against file sharing sites, which may earn revenues from advertising by offering an abundance of content. Legal notices are served against sites to take down unauthorized copies, but this is not a war which is going to end any time soon. There have been actions to block access to websites such as Pirate Bay, with ISPs being asked to restrict access, and also search engines have downgraded these sites so that they do not appear prominently in search results.

Levels of piracy differ between countries, and for example Russia seems to experience high levels of piracy for books. Ebook readers are a common sight if you travel on the Moscow Metro but few of the books being read will have been purchased. Some estimates suggest that pirated books account for 90 per cent of downloads, and that around 100,000 titles are available, including books translated illegally.[37] This can only have a detrimental impact on book sales, both pbooks and ebooks, with the category of fiction experiencing a drop of around 30 per cent by 2012.[38] In 2012 Oleg Novikov, head of the Eksmo publishing company, warned that without greater protection from the government 'authors would stop writing altogether and find another way to make money'.[39]

64 Content in a digital world

As we saw in an earlier chapter, there are some authors who are happy to be pirated on the basis that their sales will increase as a result of the wider exposure. Paulo Coelho wrote encouragement of piracy on his blog: 'Pirates of the world, unite and pirate everything I've ever written!'[40] If you hear a song on the radio, it makes you want to go and buy the CD, and Coelho believes it is the same with literature. He was writing in response to the Stop Online Piracy Act, a bill put before the US Congress in 2011, designed to increase the power of companies to take action against both infringing sites and ISPs and search engines which allow access or effectively promote those sites. In response, in January 2012, Wikipedia and other websites staged a blackout of their services to highlight the threat they saw posed by the bill to both free speech and innovation.

Other authors, however, are less sanguine about the dangers of piracy. The Spanish bestselling writer Lucia Etxebarria, who won the Planeta Prize in 2004, announced in 2011 that she had been defeated by online piracy. Her country was at the top of the world rankings for per capita illegal downloads, and this was reflected in her discovery that her sales had been overtaken by the downloading of illegal copies of her books. She decided to throw in the towel and give up writing books altogether. In 2012 the fantasy author Terry Goodkind self-published a new ebook exclusive, *The First Confessor: The legend of Magna Searus*. Goodkind was dismayed to find pirated editions available soon after, and went on the offensive. He named one of the pirates, with a photo, on his Facebook page, and wrote: 'How ironic you claim to be a fan of books that uphold truth and honour above all else. We hope the price of fame is worth the cost of your infamy.'[41] The pirates quickly withdrew in the face of such an onslaught, and Goodkind could claim victory.

Adrian Johns, in his book on the history of piracy, says that its story has two implications.[42] First that intellectual property only exists as long as it is recognized and defended; second that measures taken against piracy can sometimes impinge upon other, equally valued, aspects of society. For the system of copyright to survive, authors, publishers, and a range of other companies and institutions have to be ready to take practical action against those seeking to undermine it. The problem today is that measures necessary to combat piracy have come to seem merely to defend the interests of the media corporations, which have pressed for action from governments and technology intermediaries. Furthermore, some of the measures proposed to control the internet, including blocking websites at the domain level, start to appear reminiscent of those carried out by totalitarian regimes. Wielding such power poses a threat to free speech. As media are consumed more and more on devices which are regularly updated by their manufacturers (think of software updates to a smartphone), and in essence still under their control – Jonathan Zitrain calls these tethered devices – then the likelihood of intervention increases further.[43]

Digital rights management (DRM)

Technology companies would argue that there is a trade-off between functionality and control. So-called 'walled gardens', closed ecosystems such as Facebook, offer a better user experience as a result of the restrictions imposed on non-approved applications or content. With ebooks consumers have faced issues around being locked into platforms (such as the Kindle format or Apple devices) and also not being able to transfer books easily between devices. The movement to issue ebooks DRM-free has been growing steadily, and for example the publisher O'Reilly offers their ebooks in several formats, with the consumer getting ownership for life. When the Pottermore site was launched in 2012, making available for the first time ebooks of the Harry Potter novels, the decision was taken not to have strict DRM in place. Instead watermarking is used, which assigns to the file details about the book and the purchaser, enabling tracking to take place. Under the terms of the agreement a purchaser can download an ebook up to eight times, allowing it to be downloaded in different formats and to different devices.[44] When a book appears on free download sites, the watermarking enables Pottermore to trace the original culprit (unless the watermarking has been stripped out). This so-called social DRM also uses the court of public opinion to enforce the original licence. It is said that one-third of piracy will happen anyway, one-third may be through ignorance, and one-third can be converted into sales. The open release of DRM controls can help build trust with a community of readers. At the same time no one would like to be shamed for having passed on their copy of the book, and the watermarking helps to make their name public. This, however, would not prevent the more limited sharing of ebooks amongst family and friends, in a similar way to the sharing of music.

Social DRM carries an echo of an earlier battle over piracy. In May 1965 the US publisher Ace Books issued an unauthorized paperback edition of Tolkien's *The Lord of the Rings*, claiming that the title had entered the public domain. The authorized edition, from Ballantine Books, appeared later in the year, with the following statement from the author: 'This paperback edition, and no other, has been published with my consent and co-operation. Those who approve of courtesy (at least) to living authors will purchase it and no other.' A campaign by the author and his readers led to a climbdown by Ace Books, who paid the author royalties and did not reprint their edition.[45]

Watermarking offers consumers of ebooks the opportunity to share their books in the same way they do their printed copies. But the ease of sharing of digital files prompts anxiety amongst publishers as to the extent to which sharing could take place. Also, what if a second-hand market in ebooks develops, and users can easily sell on their licence to a digital book?[46]

Widely known is the theory of Six Degrees of Separation, whereby two people can be connected with each other through a series of intermediary steps. This in turn spawned the game Six Degrees of Kevin Bacon, in which players have to link a movie actor with Kevin Bacon in as few steps as possible. The idea originates from the 1960s, when psychologist Stanley Milgram conducted a study using communication by letter to find out how many steps it would take to link two separate individuals. He set out to investigate the phenomenon of 'The Small-World Problem', whereby when two strangers fall into conversation they often come up with an acquaintance in common:

66 Content in a digital world

> many people were surprised to learn that only five intermediaries will, on the average, suffice to link any two randomly chosen individuals, no matter where they happen to live in the United States. ... Elements of geometrical progression with an increase rate far more powerful than mere doubling underlie the small world search procedure.[47]

A study of Facebook users carried out in 2011 (at that time Facebook users represented one-tenth of the world's population) revealed that 92 per cent were connected by only four intermediaries, and when the analysis was limited to a single country, the number of intermediaries dropped to only three.[48] In essence social media is making the world an even smaller place. This can be used to advantage to spread memes around the world, but also demonstrates why publishers are nervous of ebooks circulating without any controls.

In the case of music, controls were implemented to limit its distribution, and there were restrictions on copying and which machines could be used to play the music. But in the end DRM was felt to be too heavy handed an approach, and when Apple eased DRM controls on iTunes in 2009, this enabled users to play their music not only on their iPod but also transfer it between computers and mobile phones.

But the release of DRM controls is separate from the ownership of content, which was brought into further prominence in 2012 when the actor Bruce Willis made the news with his alleged realization that he could not leave his downloaded music to his children. Mic Wright observed:

> You have the right to transfer it to other devices and make copies for yourself, but the extent that you actually own those songs is tricky. You own a right to play them and copy them but giving them to others is not covered. That's where Bruce Willis has started to worry about what happens when he dies hardest.[49]

The Bruce Willis conundrum highlights an important difference in the ownership of physical and digital copies of copyrighted works.

The future of copyright

When you buy a printed book, it is yours to pass on to friends and family, or to take down to the second-hand shop or charity shop. You can leave it on your shelf and find it again in 30 years' time. Under what is called the first sale doctrine, the original copyright owner's interest is exhausted after the book's initial purchase, although you are prohibited from making a further copy yourself. By contrast, if you download a digital book, most likely you are only acquiring it under a licence. You do not own the content and you can only pass it on to others if the licence so allows. There is the famous example of book purchasers in 2009 who had downloaded the novel *1984* to read on their Kindle, only to find it withdrawn when

Amazon realized there was a problem regarding the rights. The irony was not lost on many, and it brought home the fact that a book could be deleted from the device even whilst being read.[50] To be absolutely sure of owning a book, you still have to buy it in print. As the Slovenian academic Miha Kovač says, 'All the books which I want to keep, I by default buy them in print, because if Amazon goes bust, all my ebooks will disappear most likely.'[51]

The principle of fair use varies in different countries and is most strongly protected in educational contexts – coming back to the idea that knowledge is a public good. Copyrighted material can be reproduced, for example, for the purposes of commentary or parody. In broad terms, limited quotation from other works is allowed without the copyright owner's permission, with use of images or more extended passages requiring permission (and perhaps payment). Where the balance should lie is open to some interpretation, and for example quoting even short extracts from poetry in copyright is more than likely to require permission. But when the use of an epigraph to open a chapter is now considered dangerous, unless the quotation is the subject of some academic discussion, surely the balance has shifted too far away from the principle of fair use? In 2012 a pub in Southampton in the UK, The Hobbit, received a letter threatening legal action from the California company which owns the worldwide rights to brands associated with Tolkien. The pub was requested to remove all references to the Tolkien books and its characters – for example, it has a range of cocktails such as the Frodo and Gandalf. After the intervention of prominent stars from the Tolkien films – Ian McKellen (Gandalf himself) and Stephen Fry – the company backed down and suggested that a licensing fee of only $100 could bring an end to the dispute.[52]

Do we also need a more flexible approach to collaborative works, to ensure their wider distribution? Digital projects can have a high level of interactivity, and can attract contributions and images from many users or participants – how do you then solve the issues around their commercialization and ownership? How do you deal with issues around copyright and moral rights, when the whole point may be to mash-up content from many different sources? Crowdsourced projects, involving many collaborators, can be fun to put together but there may be difficulties in tracking down contributors and gaining their permission to publish. This can be an elaborate process for publishers wishing to commercialize a project from a number of sources. But if the collaboration is not for commercial gain, should the copyright regime not be more tolerant? The issue is one of motive, and this can be easy or hard to discern. The online photo sharing company, Instagram, which is owned by Facebook, caused a furore in 2012 when it set out to commercialize its content through changing its terms and conditions. It wanted to be able to sell images to advertisers without any further permission and without passing on any share of the payment to the owners of the images. The subsequent uproar led Instagram to back down, and state that it was not trying to claim ownership of the content. But the intent was clear – the company needed to find ways to make money from its free online service.[53]

68 Content in a digital world

Another area of collaboration is the scanlation of manga: 'a scanlator is a person or group of people who work collaboratively to scan and then translate manga so that fans all around the world can enjoy them.'[54] Fans of manga who want to share the latest publications from Japan post their own digital editions of the books with varying degrees of primitiveness, depending on the source material. They may be preparing unauthorized editions, but this subculture partly came about in response to the slow publication process in Western markets for sourcing authentic editions. Such a motivation is reflected in the general view of most scanlation groups that they should not pirate works that are under licence in international markets:

> Another influential norm is that when a manga is licensed its scanlation and distribution [are] stopped. Although there are groups who are not tightly bound by this norm, many participants tend to regard it as an important criterion that distinguishes scanlation from illegal file-sharing. Scanlators are alerted to, and generally have a good knowledge of, license deals in the industry.[55]

Although manga sales in the USA peaked in 2007, the industry was not particularly concerned about the effects of scanlation. Publishers were reluctant to take legal action since this might hurt their fan base, and word of mouth around scanlated titles could spur publishers to license particular series, and for those books to sell well. Often readers might want to purchase physical copies of their favourite titles.

The artist Tracey Emin participated in a project with a primary school in London in 2000, whereby children came up with words around the theme of 'Tell Me Something Beautiful'. The words were then sewn into a quilt, and the school exhibited the work. When later on the school tried to sell the work as by Tracey Emin, the artist argued both that the work was not one of hers but also that she wanted it back. The dispute was settled by the school agreeing to keep it and put it on display. Properly, in order to be the subject of a commercial sale, the work should have been subject to a written agreement at the time of its creation, but of course the school would barely have been aware of such a need when the project was originally started. It is also unlikely that they set out to create the quilt to make money.

Do we have the right duration of copyright in place at the moment? In 1841 Lord Macaulay observed in a speech that copyright is a 'tax on readers for the purpose of giving a bounty to writers'.[56] He viewed a long, posthumous term of copyright as nonsensical, giving the example of Dr Johnson, who died in 1784:

> Would the knowledge that this copyright would exist in 1841 have been a source of gratification to Johnson? Would it have stimulated his exertions? Would it have once drawn him out of his bed before noon? Would it have once cheered him under a fit of the spleen? ... Considered as a reward to him, the difference between a twenty years' and sixty years' term of posthumous copyright would have been nothing or next to nothing.

Under the Sonny Bono Copyright Term Extension Act (1998), the copyright term in the United States was extended, from life plus 50 years, by another 20 years. The Act was also known as the Mickey Mouse Act because lobbying by Disney contributed to the decision that for works for hire, for example movies, the term was extended to an astonishing 95 years. *Mickey Mouse*, first copyrighted in 1928, remains in copyright until 2023.

The long term of copyright surely cannot be justified as an incentive to creative production, and it also has had the disadvantage of creating a no-man's land of works in copyright which are not readily available. A work may languish, forgotten and perhaps rightly so, but there is no incentive for a publisher to bring it back into print if the rights holder cannot easily be traced. These so-called orphan works have become more of an issue in recent years with the digitization of millions of books by Google. They have digitized the books from copyright libraries such as the Bodleian in Oxford, with the aim of making them readily available on the web. There was no issue over books out of their term of copyright, but problems arose when they also digitized out-of-print books still in copyright. They argued that under the principle of fair use, it was permissible to make these books available. This became a matter of dispute with both authors and publishers, who argued that Google were infringing copyright by not obtaining the necessary permission. Books still in print with publishers were made available under arrangements made with the companies.

Provisions were made by Google to compensate rights holders through a mechanism of the Registry, which would pay out 63 per cent of receipts from, for example, the sale of individual titles or advertising. As Michael Healy points out, the Settlement would have provided a useful mechanism for making available orphan works, rather than see them disappear from view.[57] In the end the legal wrangles meant that the Registry was never put in place. The proposed establishment of a Digital Copyright Hub in the UK would create a similar registry, enabling use of a copyrighted work, in return for a suitable fee, where it is hard to establish the identity of the present rights holder. By the end of 2012, the dispute between publishers and Google was resolved through agreement that publishers could choose which titles could be digitized; but the dispute with authors had still not been settled, nor the issue of how orphan works should be handled.[58]

Moving to a shorter term of copyright would enable books to be made freely available much sooner, without preventing authors from enjoying financial rewards from their works during their lifetime. A report was commissioned into the economic effects of the US copyright extension, which suggested that only 2 per cent of copyrights, once they were between 55 and 75 years old, still had commercial value. In effect there was additional income accruing to copyright holders who had already earned a good income from the works.

There is a further suggestion that intellectual property should be viewed as a public good. It can be enjoyed by as many people as possible, just like the air we breathe, and so should be freely available. This argument is given further weight with the growth of digital media, where the marginal cost of a further user is close

70 Content in a digital world

to zero. The report into the copyright extension examined this idea and how it can be brought into practice:

> intellectual property can be characterized as a public good, meaning that use of the knowledge or aesthetic concepts does not deplete them; use incurs no marginal cost. Clearly, though, not allowing any charge for use of a copyright would mean no compensation to the creator and would fail to achieve the purpose of providing an incentive to create. As a compromise solution society has chosen the principle of monopoly for a limited time.[59]

A shorter term of copyright would not significantly disadvantage copyright holders but would encourage renewed publication of older works and their wider circulation. A more flexible approach to collaborative works and fair use would also enable greater experimentation and creativity.

Notes

1. Peter Jaszi, 'Toward a Theory of Copyright: The metamorphoses of "authorship"', *Duke Law Journal*, 1:2 (1991), April, page 463.
2. Lawrence Lessig, *Free Culture: How big media uses technology and the law to lock down culture and control creativity*, Penguin, 2004, page 3.
3. Ibid., page 106.
4. See http://deutsche-boerse.com – press release of 4 September 2012, accessed 5 September 2012.
5. Ashley Rawlings and Craig Mod, *Art Space Tokyo: An intimate guide to the Tokyo art world*, Pre-post, 2010, page iv.
6. Stewart Brand (ed.), 'Keep Designing: How the information economy is being created and shaped by the hacker ethic', *Whole Earth Review* (1985), May, page 49.
7. Kevin Kelly, 'Scan this Book!', *New York Times*, 14 May 2006.
8. Mira T. Sundara Rajan, *Moral Rights: Principles, practice and new technology*, Oxford University Press, 2011, page 7.
9. See ibid., pages 61–3. It is interesting to reflect on whether *Pride and Prejudice and Zombies* (see chapter 1) would be seen as a violation of the author's enduring moral rights.
10. Tim Bradshaw, 'UK CD Sales Slump to Half of 2004 Peak', *Financial Times*, 2 January 2012.
11. Ben Sisario, 'Full Album Sales Showed a Little Growth in 2011', *New York Times*, 4 January 2012.
12. Dave Lee, 'A Glimpse at Piracy in the UK and Beyond', 17 September 2012, http://www.bbc.co.uk/news/technology-19599527, accessed 19 September 2012.
13. Eric Pfanner, 'Copyright Cheats Face the Music in France', *New York Times*, 19 February 2012.
14. Adrian Adermon and Che-Yuan Liang, 'Piracy, Music and Movies: A natural experiment', IFN Working Paper, No. 854, 2010, Research Institute of Industrial Economics, Stockholm, Sweden.
15. 'Where do Music Collections Come From?', blog posted on the American Assembly, Columbia University, http://piracy.americanassembly.org/where-do-music-collections-come-from/, accessed 19 October 2012.
16. See http://blogs.tn.com.ar/internet/archives/2008/06/joss_stone_y_la_pirateria_en_la_red.html, accessed 23 September 2013.

17 Patrik Wikström, *The Music Industry: Music in the cloud*, Polity Press, 2009, page 137.
18 Joel Waldfogel, 'Is the Sky Falling? The quality of new recorded music since Napster', column posted at Vox, 14 November 2011, http://www.voxeu.org/, accessed 29 February 2012.
19 Interviewed in the *Observer*, 24 February 2013.
20 Jeremy Denk, 'Flight of the Concord: The perils of the recording studio', *New Yorker*, 6 February 2012.
21 Paul Steinle and Sara Brown, 'Embracing the Future', *American Journalism Review*, Spring 2012, page 52.
22 Pew Research Center's Project for Excellence in Journalism, *The State of the News Media 2012*, Key Findings. Available at http://stateofthemedia.org/2012/overview-4/key-findings/, accessed 12 July 2012.
23 Dean Starkman, 'Major Papers' Longform Meltdown', *Columbia Journalism Review*, 17 January 2013. Available at http://www.cjr.org/the_audit/major_papers_longform_melt-down.php?page=all, accessed 26 February 2013.
24 'Who Killed the Newspaper?', *The Economist*, 24 August 2006.
25 Clay Shirky, 'The Times' Paywall and Newsletter Economics', http://www.shirky.com/weblog/2010/11/the-times-paywall-and-newsletter-economics/, accessed 22 February 2012. He references a piece on Nicholas Carr's blog, 'Google in the middle', dated 10 April 2009, http://www.roughtype.com/archives/2009/04/google_in_the_m.php, accessed 22 February 2012.
26 Pew Research Center's Project for Excellence in Journalism, *The State of the News Media 2012*, Major Trends. Available at http://stateofthemedia.org/2012/overview-4/major-trends/, accessed 12 July 2012.
27 Giles Tremlett, 'Spain's El País Newspaper Feels the Pain as it Axes One Third of Workforce', *Guardian*, 14 October 2012.
28 Dietmar Henning, 'German Newspapers Call for Pay Cuts', 17 May 2011, World Socialist Web Site, http://www.wsws.org/articles/2011/may2011/germ-m17.shtml, accessed 19 October 2012.
29 Ken Auletta, 'Citizens Jain: Why India's newspaper industry is thriving', *New Yorker*, 8 October 2012.
30 Ian Hargreaves, *Digital Opportunity: A review of intellectual property and growth*, page 6. Available at http://www.ipo.gov.uk/ipreview, accessed 23 September 2013.
31 Stephen Mesquita, 'Trends in Travel Publishing in the US and UK markets', *Logos*, 22:3 (2011), pages 44–50.
32 See the interview with Lewis DVorkin, Chief Product Officer of Forbes Media, *Guardian*, 22 April 2013.
33 Chris Anderson, *Free: The Future of a Radical Price: The economics of abundance and why zero pricing is changing the face of business*, Random House, 2009.
34 Mira T. Sundara Rajan, *Moral Rights: Principles, practice and new technology*, Oxford University Press, 2011, page 494. The term 'open access' has most prominence in the area of academic publishing, where it is argued that publicly funded research should be made freely available to all.
35 Ibid., page 502.
36 Wendy Cope, 'You like my poems? So pay for them', *Guardian*, 8 December 2007.
37 Peter Mountford, 'Steal My Book! Why I'm abetting a rogue translation of my novel', *The Atlantic* (2012), November. Available at http://www.theatlantic.com/magazine/archive/2012/11/steal-my-book/309105/, accessed 28 November 2012.
38 Statistic about fiction sales from Publishers Association International Conference, London, 13 December 2012.
39 'Executive Urges Intellectual Property Protection', *Moscow Times*, 24 April 2012.
40 Paulo Coelho, 'My Thoughts on SOPA', entry in his blog, 20 January 2012, http://paulocoelhoblog.com/2012/01/20/welcome-to-pirate-my-books/, accessed 28 October 2012.

72 Content in a digital world

41 Alison Flood, 'Book "Pirate" Goes Underground after being Named by Terry Goodkind', *Guardian*, 11 July 2012.
42 Adrian Johns, *Piracy: The Intellectual property wars from Gutenberg to Gates*, University of Chicago Press, 2009, pages 497–8.
43 Jonathan Zittrain, *The Future of the Internet: And how to stop it*, Yale University Press, 2008.
44 See http://www.pottermore.com/
45 See Christina Scull and Wayne G. Hammond, *The J. R. R. Tolkien Companion and Guide*, HarperCollins, 2006.
46 Such a service, ReDigi, existed for music until a US federal court ruled in 2013 that the business model infringed copyright. The company argued that the first sale doctrine – see the section below – applied but in fact most music is supplied under a licence. Ben Sisario, 'A Setback for Resellers of Digital Products', *New York Times*, 1 April 2013.
47 Stanley Milgram, 'The Small-World Problem', *Psychology Today*, 1:1 (1967), May, page 66.
48 Lars Backstrom, 'Anatomy of Facebook', Facebook Data Science, 21 November 2011, http://www.facebook.com/notes/facebook-data-science/anatomy-of-facebook/10150388519243859, accessed 19 October 2012.
49 Mic Wright, 'Bruce Willis versus Apple: Do we own what we download?', *Telegraph* blog, http://blogs.telegraph.co.uk/technology/micwright, accessed 5 September 2012.
50 Brad Stone, 'Amazon Erases Orwell Books From Kindle', *New York Times*, 18 July 2009.
51 Interviewed by the author, 23 January 2013.
52 'The Hobbit Pub could be Saved after Gandalf Stepped in to Help', *Daily Telegraph*, 16 March 2012.
53 Jenna Wortham, 'Facebook Responds to Anger Over Proposed Instagram Changes', *New York Times*, 18 December 2012.
54 Definition from the Baka-Updates website, http://www.mangaupdates.com/groups.html, accessed 24 September 2013.
55 Hye-Kyung Lee, 'Between Fan Culture and Copyright Infringement: Manga scanlation', *Media, Culture & Society*, 31:6 (2009), page 1017.
56 Thomas Babington Macaulay, *Speeches on Copyright*, edited by Charles Gaston, Ginn, 1914, page 25.
57 Michael Healy, 'The Google Book Settlement: The end of the long and winding road?', *Logos*, 22:4 (2011).
58 In November 2013 a New York court ruled in favour of Google's argument that the digitization programme constituted fair use.
59 Edward Rappaport, 'Copyright Term Extension: Estimating the economic values', Congressional Research Service, Library of Congress, 11 May 1998, page 2.

4

DIGITAL CAPITAL

As digital books are bought and read, and substituted for print sales and ownership of those books, what challenges does this bring about for the way in which we consume books? Where will the value be created and held in this new world? What forms of capital are important in a digital environment? As bookstores disappear from the high street, how will we discover new books and authors? How will books be packaged and sold in an online environment? Do we actually need to own books any longer?

There is no doubt about the disruption felt in the industry. Alongside the arrival of ebooks in the market, the publishing industry has had to contend with the growth of free, often user-generated, content available online. The internet is the default option for obtaining information – the share of search held by Google has been around 90 per cent – and users are using a range of websites to find relevant content, from Facebook and Wikipedia to TripAdvisor and IMDb. Offline brands have not necessarily transferred successfully online, and for many publishers it has been their author brands which have been most prominent rather than their imprints.

The publishing industry has conducted experiments in digital publishing since the early 1990s with, in turn, CD-Roms and online publishing. The latter took hold in areas such as journals and professional publishing. What changed the consumer publishing industry was the interest taken by the large technology players in how books are bought and read. Sony, who revolutionized the music market with the original Walkman, came out with a reader in 2006 with the proud tagline: 'Finally, the digital book has come of age'. The ereader did not break open the market, partly because it lacked the associated range of content to meet the expectations of consumers, but the device did much to make people comfortable with the idea of reading books on a screen. Microsoft began a book digitization programme in 2005, in what looked like a copy of the initiative by Google. Their

74 Digital capital

avowed aim was to improve online search by converting offline content – initially books in the public domain. They abandoned the project in 2008, claiming that it was more important to develop a sustainable business model for search. A few eyebrows were raised in 2012 when they announced a collaboration with the US chain Barnes & Noble to create a strategic partnership in the area of digital reading.

Apple is also a surprise player in the market for books, given that Steve Jobs said in 2008 of the Kindle: 'It doesn't matter how good or bad the product is, the fact is that people don't read anymore. Forty per cent of the people in the US read one book or less last year. The whole conception is flawed at the top because people don't read anymore.'[1] But advertising for the iPad continues to feature reading books as one of the tablet's benefits, and before his death Jobs was making plans to break open the textbook market. A further irony was that the biography of Jobs by Walter Isaacson proved to be an international bestseller.

Google entered the market with its digitization programme, launched in 2004, converting out of copyright works but also more controversially works where the copyright holder could not be traced. It also worked with publishers to display part of or the whole text, to enable sales of in-print books. It is now selling books alongside other media from its Google Play store, and is competing in the device market alongside both Apple and Amazon.

Google's work with books has undoubtedly raised the quality of their search capability, by adding these texts into their database. Sergey Brin, one of the two founders of Google, said that the comprehensiveness of a search is not just about the number of words or bytes: 'It's about having the really high-quality information. You have thousands of years of human knowledge, and probably the highest-quality knowledge is captured in books.'[2] The books database is also contributing to their research in the area of artificial intelligence, and the development of their Google Translate service.

Although there are other players in the ebook market, such as Kobo, the big beast is Amazon, with a high market share first in print and now especially in ebooks. The giant retailer began its operations with books back in 1995, as Jeff Bezos identified the benefits that internet retailing would bring to customers in this market by offering not just products but also a service: a large choice of titles, far more than could possibly be available in even the biggest superstore; 24/7 availability and convenience, in particular for those without a local bookstore; and personalization around the customer's interests. The ebook market did not open up for Amazon until they got the device right and with the Kindle they produced a high-quality reading experience with the advantages of portability, low prices, and virtually instant access to a host of content (over 1.3 million titles in 2012). Jeff Bezos had declared the book to be the 'last bastion of analog', and again he got the service element right with the Kindle – a seamless operation backed with enough content and competitive pricing of individual titles.[3]

An examination of the factors that encourage increasing numbers of consumers to shop online – and the arrival of ebooks is an extension of this shift – shows why books are amongst the products most readily bought online. Overall it is convenience and price that drive online retail; variety and product information are much less important.[4] In some categories, such as groceries, consumers still largely to prefer to shop instore, where they can see some products first hand. By contrast people are more comfortable about shopping for books, music, and film online, and they seem happy that they know the product and do not need to see it for themselves. There are also plenty of opportunities to view sample content. Consumers will choose the right channel – online, bricks and mortar, TV shopping, mobile – according to what works best for an occasion or type of purchase. A study of online shopping found that 'Staggeringly, more than 90% of global online shoppers buy books, music and films, clothing and footwear online.'[5] Also of interest for the future was that around one-third of respondents in the USA were using social media to follow consumer brands or retailers. They were not yet using social media to shop but it can be seen as a source of information and influence.[6]

Digital disruption

Why has it taken external players to shake up book publishing? If the industry could see what had happened in photography or music, why did publishers and booksellers not embrace ebooks and a digital future? Well firstly they had a secure business model which worked – the printed book – and there was no reason to change. There was also a system of physical distribution which worked reasonably well – albeit with some inefficiencies. Physical bookstores offered a browsing experience, and the internet facilitated sales of slower-selling titles which would not necessarily be stocked in the high street. There had been experiments with ebooks but until the right device came along, sales were low and no one could see anyone reading a whole book on a PC. There had been excursions into the CD-Rom market with multimedia products in the 1990s but the high development costs were rarely recouped. In any case, as many commentators concluded, the printed book was a technology which had survived a long time and was unlikely to be improved upon. Encouraging the production of digital content would also lay the industry open to its 'napsterization' with freely available, pirated content.

But if we can see it now – that ebooks can work – why not before? Clayton Christensen, who has studied disruption across many industries, does not see it as an issue of bad management. Simply it is very hard for companies to disrupt themselves – why would they countenance such an action? Going into new markets in their infancy hardly seems sensible when there are profits to be made in established markets. Disruptive products are usually cheaper, and it sounds like the companies will achieve lower profit margins. It would also have been difficult for a single player to aggregate the required content across the whole market. Without some form of co-operation between the existing players in the market, it needed an external party to source the content and then offer the device and the

76 Digital capital

appropriate service for the market. This is what Apple did with music, and Amazon put the pieces together to break open the market for ebooks.

One of the businesses studied by Christensen was the steel industry in the USA. Minimill steel-making first became commercially viable in the 1960s and by the mid-1990s it was the most efficient and cost-effective part of the industry. This involved making steel in new plants which were one-tenth of the scale of the larger, established plants – they were called integrated mills. Yet none of the major players had built their own plants, persisting with their higher-cost, capital-intensive plants. The share of steel output taken by the minimills grew from zero in 1965 to 40 per cent in 1995. Why then did the larger producers not react when they could quite clearly see how the market was changing? Firstly the early steel produced in the smaller plants was of lower quality, and captured what was known as the rebar market – steel reinforcing bars. The larger producers were almost relieved not to have to compete in this part of the market, content to produce in the area of higher-quality steel with higher profit margins. For example they made steel for cans or the car industry. But over time the minimills started to move upmarket and capture other parts of the market, such as structural beams. Again the larger mills were content to concentrate on the higher tiers of the market, convincing themselves that a higher rate of return is the ultimate goal. They were highly reluctant to disrupt their own market, and retreating to parts of the market where they did not have to compete with the minimills seemed the right option.

This has also been the case with ebooks, where the established publishers were not the first to disrupt the market – it was the technology players. Indeed some publishers were slow to enter the ebook market even when the signs of change were there. As Christensen says: 'In the tug-of-war for development resources, projects targeted at the explicit needs of current customers or at the needs of existing users that a supplier has not yet been able to reach will always win over proposals to develop products for markets that do not exist.'[7] Also a disruptive technology is often embraced by the least profitable customers in a market – this is the case with ebooks in a market where many consumers are downloading books for free or at $0.99. Christensen sees the dangers of simply relying on the needs of consumers to stick with an existing technology: 'products that do not appear to be useful to our customers today (that is, disruptive technologies) may squarely address their needs tomorrow'.[8] It just didn't look like the market needed ebooks – or that consumers were even interested – in the early days: the evidence was there in the low level of sales. But of course when the devices improved and came down in price, and the range of available titles expanded sufficiently, consumers worked out the benefits of an ereader and started telling their friends and buying them as presents. Could self-published works be the equivalent of the rebar market, eating away at the lower end of the scale? The lower entry costs in the books industry – for example, there is no longer the requirement to invest in warehousing of physical stock – will continue to attract new players. There is also scope for further disruption amongst book categories beyond linear fiction, which may require different kinds of expertise in, say, video production. Mike Shatzkin says:

I am agnostic, I am sceptical about whether all things that have been books for the last one hundred or two hundred years will (a) map into the future as discrete products; and (b), if they do whether book publishers have anything particular to contribute. I think that the disruption we have seen so far could be just the overture.[9]

Discoverability

For the traditional bricks-and-mortar bookstores, the challenge has been to reinvent yourself or die. In a world where consumers are content to buy even shoes and clothes online, can the appeal of the physical bookstore and its browsing experience be maintained? Can you build a relationship with your customers, so that they remain loyal? For independents this means operating in specific subject areas (e.g. travel or LGBT), as an active player in the local community, hosting events, and adding on other services – for example, a coffee shop or activities for children. How do you cater for an audience when the market includes ebooks? Barnes & Noble in the USA made some headway with building a digital experience instore, and the success of Apple stores suggests there is still a need for a physical presence even for digital products. But with ebooks eating away at your sales, it is difficult to see physical bookstores surviving in the longer term. Profit margins are thin enough already if you are occupying a visible location on the high street and maintaining decent stock levels. Although the number of independent bookstores in the USA rose slightly from 2009 to 2012, around 1,000 had gone out of business from 2000 to 2007, and book retail lost another 650 shops with the closure of the Borders chain in 2011.[10]

The music industry, which has faced a similar situation, has seen a rapid decline in the number of record shops, both independent and chain. Graham Jones wrote about the situation in the UK in his book, *Last Shop Standing* (2009). Shockingly, at the beginning of the book, he lists over 500 independent stores which had closed in the previous four years. He doesn't think there is no future at all for music independents but the picture is certainly bleak. When he looks at the shops which have survived, they are in towns not cities, away from the main high street (to ensure rents are lower), and relying on regular customers rather than passing trade. They need to sell physical products which offer more than what is available through a simple download. These include vinyl and limited edition titles – collectable by fans – perhaps with a code to enable the fan to download the music as well. The shops also need to appeal to customers with diverse tastes, looking for more obscure genres.

One second-hand music shop which closed, Beanos in Croydon, issued a final statement to the world from its owner (in 2009):

> Only ten years ago we were the leading second-hand record dealer in the world. … Then along came eBay. Then along came Amazon. Then along came 'downloading'. Then along came the time when it was no longer

78 Digital capital

necessary to actually possess anything musical. Nothing tangible, like an LP cover, or even a CD-insert with some possibly interesting information. Nothing to file. Nothing to show off to friends. No, now your life can be on an iPod or a phone. Your music, your photos, your contacts. 'Imagine no possessions,' as John Winston Lennon once said.[11]

When the old and familiar structures in the market disappear, a whole set of new issues arise. Publishers traditionally published the hardback, perhaps a large-format paperback, and then a smaller, mass market paperback. They changed their structures to achieve vertical integration within the same company. There were set norms around the relevant price points, and the books had to be packaged up into one part of the market: for example, popular science, literary fiction, or travel writing. Covers would be created with the particular part of the market in mind. Publicity and marketing would lead up to the publication date, and encourage instore display, sell through, and a buzz amongst the relevant types of readers.

If physical bookstores are disappearing, how does a reader find a new book, author, or some unexpected choice?[12] Evidence from the USA suggests that the percentage of impulse purchases is much lower for online book sales compared to purchases in physical bookstores (11 per cent as against 26 per cent).[13] Will such sales vanish or be replaced by safer choices? There is certainly a multitude of choice online, but how can readers navigate this territory? They can look at bestseller lists but the factor of serendipity, welcomed by many, will disappear. Can it be satisfactorily replaced by some random generator of titles, or will personalized recommendations, based on past browsing and reading behaviour, suffice? Just as bricks-and-mortar stores are happy to receive incentives to display titles more prominently, any recommendations system is also open to abuse. The issue is that whilst books are increasingly bought online, they are not necessarily being discovered there. A study in 2013 found that whereas 61 per cent of purchases by frequent book buyers took place online, only 7 per cent of those buyers had discovered the book online.[14]

This issue of discoverability is not simply confined to books. In 2012 there were around 700,000 apps available for the iPhone and iPad, with hundreds more added each day. This product range helps to sell the hardware, but offers little prospect of success for the app writers working in such an overcrowded field. Apple itself highlights some apps but most remain largely invisible, not being open to web searches in the manner of websites. App developers (or appreneurs) are competing against a host of companies from a wide range of sectors, whether in film, gaming, or advertising. Ethan Nicholas got rich in 2009 with a game for the iPhone, but within only a few years, the situation had changed: 'I got lucky with iShoot, because back then a decent app could still be successful. But competition is fierce nowadays, and decent isn't good enough.'[15]

The range of book titles available online is staggering, especially compared to the tens of thousands of print books on display in a physical bookstore. Does more choice lead to better outcomes for the consumer? There is some evidence to suggest otherwise, with consumers being happier with their decisions after a more limited choice is offered. Barry Schwartz writes about the paradox of choice, whereby many of us find an abundance of choice leaves us dissatisfied:

> My concern, given the research on trade-offs and opportunity costs, is that as the number of options goes up, the need to provide justifications for decisions also increases. And though this struggle to find reasons will lead to decisions that seem right at the moment, it will not necessarily lead to decisions that feel right later on.[16]

Further, if choice is more limited, we feel less responsible for the decision, compared to the situation where there is an amazing set of products on offer. There the final decision shows up our own taste or lack of it, and the stakes become higher.

In a high street shop or online, there may be aids to help us make a decision or to narrow our set of choices. These include bestseller lists, table-top displays, staff recommends, and ratings provided by other purchasers. Some will head for these to simplify decision-making; others may run in the other direction in order to display their individuality or their disdain for the popular choices. Writing about his dissatisfaction with the ease of downloading music compared to the hunt in record shops, Mike Spies reflects on a reduction of value. Having rejected the chance to buy a CD from a flea market, since he knows he can now find all music online, he identifies a sense of loss:

> We seem to have created an environment in which wonderful music, newly discovered, is difficult to treasure. For treasures, as the fugitive salesman in the flea market was implying, are hard to come by – you have to work to find them. And the function of fugitive salesmen is to slow the endless deluge, drawing our attention to one album at a time, creating demand not for what we need to survive but for what we yearn for. Because how else can you form a relationship with a record when you're cursed with the knowledge that, just an easy click away, there might be something better, something crucial and cataclysmic? The tyranny of selection is the opposite of freedom. And the more you click, the more you enhance the disposability of your endeavor.[17]

Bookshops provide a browsing experience which it is difficult to find online. Covers may attract a potential purchaser, the book can be handled and opened at random, and a new author may just find an audience. Once a book has been picked up by a potential purchaser, they are then five times more likely to buy.[18] The challenge is to replicate this in the digital world, and create communities around content which allow readers to explore new authors. But publishers cannot direct discovery in the same way that they can in the physical environment of the bookshop, where they can if necessary buy shelf space. Mike Shatzkin comments,

80 Digital capital

'What is happening now is that people Google things, they read blog posts, they do all kinds of things which the publisher has much less control over.'[19] Already sample chapters can be downloaded, covers can be interactive, and social media offer a route for authors or publishers to reach an audience directly; and publishers are working hard on metadata for their books which will guide searches. Can users match the browsing experience to be found in a bookstore? Well, the answer is yes for many people. Some may not be in easy reach of a neighbourhood store, and others, perhaps wishing to explore the possibilities of a niche in non-fiction or a genre in fiction, will find a comprehensive choice online. Yet it is the random element which is disappearing – the chance discovery which adds to the diversity of our reading. Michael Bhaskar of Profile Books talks about digital products and the continued importance of high street shops:

> it is still very hard to market digital-only products. Without the physical presence, you do not get the same media attention, but more critically you do not have the same visibility in people's lives. ... Bookshops have become like sales agents for online retailers in that people go into the bookshop, they find the books that they want in that serendipitous way that bookshops have, and then they just go off and buy them elsewhere.[20]

Connectivity can offer the chance to monitor readers' tastes and steer them towards new writing. Amazon does this through its recommends based on customers' purchasing and browsing history. An examination of a customer's reading history may also provide opportunities, as data is available on which books have been read of those purchased. But this does smack of Big Brother – should not our reading choices and habits be private? There are also websites on which readers can post what they are reading, as well as on their Facebook pages. Chad Post, who uses such a site to see what his friends are reading, recommending, and aiming to read, spots a disadvantage: 'Recently though, I noticed that all of my friends are just like me. ... My social group doesn't necessarily inform me, it reflects back at me my own literary values.'[21]

Word of mouth

Alongside visibility to browsers in a bookshop, publishers have also relied on word of mouth (WOM) to spread advice and recommendation about books and authors. Intuitively publishers have known it is not just that bestselling titles create WOM, but that there is a positive effect on sales from one reader talking to a potential purchaser. Recommendations from friends, family, and work colleagues can drive sales; and 'what are you reading at the moment?' forms part of many casual conversations. If they could bottle the secret of this word-of-mouth buzz, publishers would, but it is not necessarily something which will go according to formula. With browsing online and the widespread use of social media, are there new routes of influence?

The evidence is that consumer reviews are a powerful driver of sales. The top two preferred sources of information about products and services, cited by over 60 per cent of US consumers in 2011, were consumer ratings and consumer reviews.[22] A study of reviews posted by consumers and their influence on book sales through online retailers showed a positive relationship between reviews and sales. The relative sales of a book were shown to be related to differences in both the number of reviews for the book and the average star ranking of the reviews. It could not be shown that reviews increased sales overall, and indeed it was possible that the pattern of reviews simply shifted sales between different titles. However the authors did conclude that because Amazon had many more reviews than other sites, this probably contributed to them having a higher market share. It is perhaps no surprise that in 2013 Amazon bought the website Goodreads, 'the world's largest site for readers and book recommendations'.[23] There was also some evidence that the relatively rare one-star reviews had a more significant, negative effect than the five-star reviews. 'This result also makes sense when the credibility of one-star and five-star reviews is considered. After all, the author, or another interested party, may "hype" his or her own book by publishing glowing reviews on these Web sites.'[24]

There have been occasions when an author intervenes to review not just their own but other, competing titles. Orlando Figes, a professor at Birkbeck College, University of London, posted reviews on Amazon under the pseudonym 'Historian'. They were negative reviews of works on Russian history and other books. Amongst the comments he offered were that the books were 'pretentious' and 'curiously dull'. Meanwhile he complimented his own book, *The Whisperers*, as 'Beautifully written ... leaves the reader awed, humbled yet uplifted ... a gift to us all'. This book, about life under Stalin, carries the description on Amazon:

> *The Whisperers* recreates the sort of maze in which Russians found themselves, where an unwitting wrong turn could either destroy a family or, perversely, later save it; a society in which everyone spoke in whispers: whether to protect themselves, their families, neighbours or friends – or to inform on them.

When confronted with his actions, Figes first denied everything, then pointed the finger at his wife in a statement issued through his lawyer, before admitting writing the derogatory reviews himself.[25] In 2012 fresh controversy arose over the existence of 'sock puppets', online personas used to write reviews, and amongst those caught indulging in the practice were publishers and the crime writer R. J. Ellory, who admitted a range of offences. It was further found that the self-published author John Locke had paid for 300 favourable reviews using a website offering such a service.[26]

Why is WOM particularly important with books rather than, say, washing machines? Well, to a great extent white goods have become commoditized with

82 Digital capital

similar levels of features and reliability. A study of product types and WOM suggested that books are highly susceptible because they are 'of great interest to many consumers or because their quality is not easy to evaluate before purchase, meaning consumers rely heavily on WOM referral'.[27] But also if you have read a book which you love, you want others to read it and share the experience. This is a key driver for WOM.

Turning to those on the receiving end of a recommendation, the degree of influence of others is a function of the receiver's involvement in the communication and the communicator's credibility. In a study of online communication, a participant said: 'Most of the time I don't bother to read the manufacturer's description, I jump immediately to other people's ratings.'[28] This is also reflected in surveys of book purchasing, where the cover blurb is not a prominent factor in either buying books or trying a new author; instead, recommendations of various types feature heavily.

For publishers, social media offer networks in which word of mouth (or word of pixel) can spread, and there are dedicated websites on which readers can share what they are reading as well as their likes and dislikes.[29] Recommendations from opinion formers on their blogs or Twitter can be invaluable. Take the example of the French writer, Laurent Binet, whose sales in English took off for his novel *HhhH* when Bret Easton Ellis took to Twitter to call it a masterpiece.[30] Blogs are regarded as a trusted form of information – ahead of advertising and email marketing – but attempts to intervene directly in the conversation can be dangerous, as users expect conversations to be open, honest, and authentic.[31] But can companies aim to create 'conversational capital'? Bertrand Cesvet thinks they can help to generate and spread positive WOM, which is important in a world where there are more choices of product than ever before, and people feel time poor. He argues that peers will talk about a product or service when the experience means something to them – they then make the consumption experience their own. When people talk about their experience of a product, they are not merely filling the gaps in the conversation, they are talking about themselves. A study of attitudes around the posting of book reviews on the internet found a high level of motivation to be involved with the product: 'consumers often made comments or remarks on the internet on the books that they were highly interested in, deeply impressed with, or about whose content they felt strongly'.[32] Becoming an advocate for a book is part of defining who you are.

It is now possible to gain insights into the conversations about books in social media, and Table 4.1 shows the top ten books attracting the most interest in social media networks towards the end of 2012.

The balance of the conversations towards a female audience fits with the profile of fiction readers, also skewed in this direction. Notable is the influence of films on the chart, and released around this time were movies of *The Hobbit*, *Life of Pi*, and *Cloud Atlas*. At the time of the release in the UK of the films, both the Tolkien and Martel titles featured in the top ten bestsellers on Amazon UK. There is a global dimension to the impact of cinema and, for example, *Life of Pi*, which had

Digital capital **83**

TABLE 4.1 Top ten books in social media, November 2012

	Book title	Author	%Male	%Female
1	The Hobbit	J. R. R. Tolkien	42	58
2	Catching Fire	Suzanne Collins	23	77
3	Life of Pi	Yann Martel	39	61
4	Fifty Shades of Grey	E.L. James	21	79
5	All In: The Education of General David Petraeus	Paula Broadwell	51	49
6	Cloud Atlas	David Mitchell	46	54
7	Mockingjay	Suzanne Collins	29	71
8	Gone Girl	Gillian Flynn	41	59
9	The Racketeer	John Grisham	53	47
10	The Elf on the Shelf: A Christmas Tradition	Carol V. Aebersold, Chanda B. Bell	14	86

Source: CoverCake chart in Publishers Weekly, 3 December 2012.

sold only 20,000 copies in China over a period of three years, sold 150,000 copies within two months of the film's release in 2012.[33]

To influence the choices of consumers and generate conversational capital, Cesvet proposes a number of engines which amplify the consumer experience.[34] These include endorsements and clearly publishers rely on these, whether for the front cover or in newspaper reviews. A celebrity endorsement, such as by Stephen Fry on Twitter, would be highly valuable. Myth is another area and, for example, Apple is built around the myth of its origins: 'The saga of Steve Jobs is the Silicon Valley creation myth writ large: launching a startup in his parents' garage and building it into the world's most valuable company.'[35] Similarly an agent or publisher will build up a story around a new author to enhance the experience. For example, 'a certain author has been picked up off the slush pile and might never have been published otherwise'. The size of the advance can also be built into the story, or the youth of the author. Take the example of Zadie Smith, who made

> an astonishing literary debut with *White Teeth* (2000). This first novel initially became notable for the publicity it received in 1997 when Smith accepted a six-figure advance for both this work, which was yet to be completed, and a future second novel. This advance is also remarkable because it was offered when she was only 21 years old and still studying English Literature at Cambridge. The publicity that arose from this commercial faith in her writing undoubtedly ensured the attention of literary critics once it was completed.[36]

Or take the area of rituals, perhaps harder to do with books, but bookshop events around publication, where readers can dress up in character, is an example. This became standard for each volume issued of the Harry Potter novels.

84 Digital capital

The arrival of ebooks offers new opportunities to rethink how to influence and create WOM effects. Self-publishing provides a narrative around which a myth can be created – this is the case with E. L. James, the author of *Fifty Shades of Grey*, who posted fan fiction on the internet before being picked up by a mainstream publisher. Cesvet talks of the opportunity to creat an EPO (exclusive product offering), giving the consumer the opportunity to own something exclusive. Just as no two music fans have the same songs and playlists on their iPod, an ereader with its selection of books becomes something special and distinctive (with lists which can be shared with friends and other readers). Users of the social media site Pinterest can pin, or repin, the covers of their favourite titles, or their favourite covers. He also talks of RSO (relevant sensory oddity), and the opportunity to make a product distinctive in form and shape. There is no reason why ebooks could not have 3D covers without the traditional rectangular borders, for example. The addition of pictures, video, and music to books is another example, which can obviously work well in some books but for fiction has mostly been found to be a distraction. An interview with the author at the end of an ebook can be a nice touch. An ereader also offers an element of privacy, and can prevent others from knowing what you are reading. This can be an advantage for some titles, for example when you are deep in a trashy thriller and not the latest literary debut. But this can also be a disadvantage when you want to impress the passenger opposite you on the train. Social media can ameliorate this effect by offering routes for everyone to know what you are reading, and can match the avenue of having your latest reading choices laid out in your sitting-room. You can tweet a passage from a book you are reading at the press of a touch screen.

Gifting of books

Many books are bought as gifts and with the growth in ebook sales, what will happen to this part of the book market? The arrival of ebook readers offers the opportunity to gift the readers themselves, and at Christmas 2011 over 1m were bought in the UK market. But in the longer run what will happen to this part of the market? Book tokens have been around since the 1930s, and gift vouchers are readily available from online stores. Will, however, the carefully chosen gift now disappear?

The value of gifts can be interpreted along four dimensions: economic, functional, social, and expressive. The first seems too calculating a dimension, if regarded as part of some *economic* exchange, and in the case of books, we rarely expect something in return for such a gift. The *functional* value might apply in the case of a guide to photography, for example, but you would assume some interest in photography on the part of the recipient. The *social* value is interpreted in terms of the network within which the giver and the recipient are placed. The social function of the gift is to 'help establish with whom, and to what degree of intimacy, social ties should be formed'.[37] The *expressive* value of the gift puts forward the idea that the gift reflects a part of the giver: 'an element of self-identity is passed on from the gift giver to the gift recipient through the gift itself'.[38] This last dimension could apply to the gift of a book you have enjoyed and are keen for a friend or family member to read. There is little economic value if you have already bought the book and simply pass it on – you may prefer for another to enjoy it rather than to keep the copy on your shelf. Alternatively you may decide to purchase additional copies to give away.

The range of books on offer, and the knowledge you have of the recipient, provide an opportunity to raise the value of the gift beyond mere money. Taking the trouble to select the right title shows an investment in time and effort which is often appreciated by the recipient – a highly appropriate choice is valued as reflecting a depth of knowledge of the other person. This is by contrast to a standardized or clichéd present.

The process of gifting can be a source of anxiety to some personality types amongst donors, and the end result the cause of disappointment to some recipients. A token or gift card can reduce the level of anxiety, and by being highly transferable, reduce the risk of disappointment. But such a choice reduces the value of the gift in the eyes of some recipients. From the point of view of the book market, a highly transferable gift, such as money or a generic token, may also divert sales elsewhere. Gifting an ebook does not suggest a high degree of involvement, by comparison to a printed book carefully selected and lovingly wrapped.

A physical copy signed by the author is an attractive self-purchase – or gift for the ardent fan – and it is also difficult to replicate this with an ebook. Fans can get their ebook reader signed on the case, and it is easy enough to insert a digital signature in the ebook. But does this match up to a signed first edition? Nicely produced physical editions, with high production values, still seem to offer many advantages to all the parties concerned in the production and purchasing of books.

Lending

The lending of books takes place between individuals – one friend passing on a book to another – and also on an institutional basis through the system of public and other libraries. The culture of lending differs between countries and for example some European countries have highly developed networks of public libraries with high usage and loan profiles.

There are severe challenges to the library system in some countries. In the UK, book acquisitions by libraries and loans showed a steady decline from 1997 to 2006. Alongside this there was a 25 per cent increase in book buying by the public, and the argument was made that the low price of books offered little incentive for buyers to use their library service. Faced with seemingly terminal decline, libraries have had to reinvent themselves from simply a place to borrow books. They have, for example, widened their stock to include DVDs and CDs. They may offer free internet access and have become more active in supporting a range of services around government, health, and education information. They support the work of

86 Digital capital

schools around children's reading, and may offer mobile services which reach more rural communities.

Despite these changes, books remain at the heart of the library offer, and a 2012 report by the Carnegie Trust highlighted the still strong relationship between being a frequent reader and library use:

> While obtaining material for reading is only one of the activities supported by public libraries, our research shows quite clearly that it is people's reading status which has the most direct bearing on whether they use the public library service and how frequently they use it. This is supported by our secondary analysis of national survey data which showed that the most common reason for using a library was to borrow or return books, while other reasons were much less common.[39]

Faced with tighter budgets for all their activities, public libraries have to marshal the arguments in their defence. Put forward is the idea that they create social capital in society – some local bookshops would also argue this case – by providing a place open to all. Libraries are spaces within which community activity can take place, and are open to a range of people otherwise excluded from a variety of information including books, newspapers, and IT access. They are important ports of call for families with children, those seeking a warm place to spend time, and being free they offer a destination without the requirement to spend any money.

Robert Putnam puts forward the central idea of social capital as that:

> networks and the associated norms of reciprocity have value … Some forms of social capital are highly formal, like a PTA (Parent-Teacher Association) organisation or a national organisation of any sort, or a labour union, formally organised with a chairman and a president, and membership dues and so on. Some forms of social capital, like the group of people who gather at the bar every Thursday evening, are highly informal.[40]

There has been much focus on changing the look and feel of library building to bring them into the twenty-first century. The series of Idea Stores, which opened in Tower Hamlets in London in the late twentieth century, were aimed at offering local residents a high-quality library service with a greater range of services, housed in attractive contemporary environments. The flagship store in Whitechapel offered:

> a fully glazed building that radiates openness and at the same time seeks to connect quite specifically with its East End surroundings. The blue and green stripes in the façade allude to the neighbourhood's market stalls, while a pedestrian walkway along the east façade of the building leads to the local supermarket and makes the building an integral part of the local shopping route. Although critics mutter darkly about the degradation of a learning

centre into an 'IKEA store', this low-threshold architecture has resulted in very high visitor numbers.[41]

A study of three public libraries in a Midwestern city in the USA found interesting dimensions to the creation of social capital. The library building 'as place' was seen as important, generating civic pride and a sense of ownership. The library offered a place of social interaction for homeless, unemployed, and single people; and it was seen as a safe place for unaccompanied children. The library served as a meeting place, and a source of resources, help, and advice. Notable were the social interactions between library staff and patrons, which established trust and ongoing relationships. 'Getting to know staff on a personal level is related to social capital, because these relationships can create a feeling of trust between the parties that makes it easier for patrons to confide their information needs to the staff member, and thus take advantage of the library's resources.'[42]

In 2013 it was announced that the first digital only library in the USA would open in Bexar County, Texas. The first of a new BiblioTech library system, it has no printed books on the shelves, and users can bring their own devices as well as borrow ereaders.[43] Although there is still a library building to be visited, in the long term we can imagine a library network which does not need a set of buildings – or perhaps even staff – to offer resources about government services and a range of general information. Ebooks can be loaned out over the internet, avoiding the necessity for patrons to leave their homes. But just as we are losing something with the disappearance of physical bookshops, we will lose a whole set of benefits for the community if we allow our library network to wither away.

Janene Cox, President of the Society of Chief Librarians in the UK, says that librarians are positive about elending:

> I think the reasons for that is that they recognise that if libraries are to remain relevant and accessible in a digital age then we have to provide our services in a way that people want to make use of them. So ebooks provide us with an opportunity for our books to be 24/7 and for people to access them remotely and for people to download them to their own digital device.[44]

An open network of lending for ebooks has dangers for the ecology of publishing, and is opposed by both authors and publishers. If a reader can access a book for free, without even leaving their home, why would they ever buy a book again? It could be argued that book purchasing has been able to prosper alongside the lending of physical books, so why not with freely available ebooks? The difference is that to borrow a physical book, you have to make the effort to visit the library and then make sure you return the copy on time. With elending potentially possible to any location, this barrier would disappear. Early experiments with ebooks, for example, found readers from China joining British libraries.[45] Do ebooks then require some built-in obsolescence, past a certain number of loans? In 2013 the idea was put forward in the UK that ebooks should deteriorate over time, leading

88 Digital capital

libraries to purchase further copies.[46] Can friction also be built into ebook lending, which mimics the wait for physical copies out on loan? This would encourage purchasing by consumers unwilling to wait their turn.

Business models

There are many business models in the media world – and constant experimentation. The value around books has shifted, away from the ownership of copyrights and licences, towards the establishment of relationships with consumers. Large technology companies have come to control this space, and publishers risk becoming simply their suppliers. Their power is limited and they are seeing prices and costs being driven down. New models of value are being created, and new channels to market. Sites which aggregate user-generated content have built value, and authors can self-publish from their own websites or work directly with retailers such as Amazon. The challenge for publishers is to work out new business models around the creation and sale of books, and to create new value around a direct relationship with consumers.

If the price of content is heading downwards, how does anyone make money along the way? This again has implications for both authors and publishers. Lindsey Davis, the former chair of the Society of Authors in the UK, says, 'When you see ebooks at 20p, that obviously is not something that can continue and allow that author to earn a living. They would have to sell millions.'[47] The large technology players have their own models with, for example, Google generating income out of advertising; Facebook from advertising and social gaming; and Amazon from a retail experience which extends from books across a host of other products. When the Kindle Fire and Paperwhite Kindle were launched in 2012, the company admitted that these were being sold at cost, with an eye to making money out of the longer-term relationship with the consumer. Looking at one month, September 2011, 33 per cent of US online users visited the Amazon website.[48]

Could advertising be the answer? In 2011 around half of US consumers said they were happy with advertising on their devices if it meant that content came free.[49] Another 2011 study found that amongst Android apps, 73 per cent were free, and of those 77 per cent relied on advertising as the main business model.[50] In the area of gaming, there are many free products which rely on advertising or payments for in-game items or upgraded versions. The latter, freemium model is designed to lure new users, who then are willing to pay for extras to get further in the game. In 2012 the *Wall Street Journal* reported:

> The strategy is gaining momentum in mobile and has become the standard model for apps, where many developers can make money from the 1% or so of people who make in-app purchases of virtual goods. About 77% of the top 100 grossing mobile apps in Apple's App Store use a freemium pricing plan, up from just 4% in 2010.[51]

The application of apps to books appears limited, for a variety of reasons. Most users will download some apps when they first get their mobile device, but over time they will not wish to clutter up their screen with a large number. For books it is simpler to download an ebook app and use this to access a wide range of content. On the supply side, with a few exceptions, publishers have made large investments in apps, only to find they have not made back their money. To a great extent they also lack the relevant competences to create multimedia. The freemium model has a limited application to book apps, and it is difficult to see what extras could be charged for, although the boundaries between games and books have become blurred. Apps have the advantage of making a book publisher seem innovative, both to authors and readers, and some big-name authors – for example cookery writers – will expect to have one prepared to accompany a new book. Overall they can be an excuse to burn a hole in the company's pocket, and enhanced ebooks can now be made relatively cheaply which closely resemble apps in their design and usability.

Freemium does seem to work in the market for books on the literature websites or mobile platforms in China. Readers have access to some chapters for free, and once they are hooked, they have to pay to find out the rest of the story. Worthy of note is that women are more willing to pay once they have reached the end of the free content; men either move on to another story or try and find the rest of the book on pirate sites.[52] There are of course some free chapters available for books in Western markets, but the Chinese model is more developed.

What about an advertising model, either in apps or ebooks? Parents are reluctant to buy apps for their children which contain advertising, and although advertising is commonly accepted in newspapers and magazines, it has been rare in books. In 2012 Yahoo filed a patent application regarding the use of ads in ebooks, citing the need for better techniques for advertising directed at ebook readers. Readers could select a level of advertising with which they are comfortable, and the greater the level of advertising, the lower the price of the book. Advertising might be related to the content of the book, and could include hyperlinks from particular words, or pictures and videos on the page.

> In some embodiments, advertising can be based on a mood and setting of content being accessed. For example, if the setting includes young characters, a Coke advertisement could be provided, inviting the reader to enjoy a glass of Coke with his or her book, and providing a graphic of a cool glass of Coke.[53]

This opens up the possibilities for product placement within novels, and although this may seem far fetched, there have been writers who have taken advantage of such opportunities. Take the example of Fay Weldon, whose novel *The Bulgari Connection* (2001) was sponsored by the Italian (now French) jeweller. Fay Weldon was unapologetic about taking the sponsorship money, and her agent wondered why it was any different from an author receiving an advance from their

90 Digital capital

publisher. Others were less impressed, and writing in the *New York Times*, Martin Arnold said:

> I leave the literary merit of the novel to the critics, but after reading the book it would appear that Ms. Weldon's problem might not be so much a matter of compromising artistic creation for commercial interests as it is awkwardness. I counted 34 mentions of Bulgari and about 15 other rhapsodies of jewelry, which in the context of the novel directly refer back to the jeweler. Mostly they stick out on the page like a boulder in the sand. For instance: '"A Bulgari necklace in the hand is worth two in the bush," said Doris.' And: 'they snuggled together happily for a bit, all passion spent; and she met him at Bulgari that lunchtime.'[54]

There are few mass audiences for advertisers amongst book readers, but the software exists to target ads at individuals. Advertising may also be less irritating for the reader as it becomes ever more narrowly focused. The 2012 presidential campaign in the USA saw sophisticated tools used to identify voters' personal interests and concerns. Cookies were employed to detect what sites were visited by voters, and then ads could be targeted with a high degree of relevance: 'If this sounds intrusive, it is. Voters get the sense they are being stalked around the internet. … I went from checking something on the Obama website to looking at high-heeled shoes at Bloomingdales.com. Since then, any time I look at shoes on any site, an Obama ad flashes up.'[55]

If we lose the bookshop experience, as such stores become rarer, some impulse sales will disappear. But will they be replaced by ad-induced impulse purchases, as our reading is tracked online or in our book choices? Amazon already has suggestions for us, based on previous purchasing and browsing – but what about based on what we read, and how much we evidently enjoy it (based on whether we finish the book and our level of absorption)? We lose the element of serendipity, but if we are choosing the level of ads we are comfortable with, we could also select an element of randomness.

We have seen already in chapter 1 how an author can use their fans to help develop plot-lines. There are new models which allow readers to take a stake in a book's publication. James Surowiecki has written about the wisdom of the crowds, and how in many instances the many are smarter than the few.[56] Can this principle apply in the early stages of a book's development? On a website such as Kickstarter, authors or publishers can make a pitch for project funding with their backers receiving differing levels of reward, from a copy of the final book to even having their likeness used for a character in a graphic novel. Projects may be multi-channel publications with development across apps, ebooks, and print. In 2012 the webcartoonist Ryan North raised a record half a million dollars for his project to turn *Hamlet* into a choose-your-own-adventure novel. He posted a new chapter online for each $5,000 the project earned and allowed readers to pick their next path. 'They chose to engage the story from the perspective of Ophelia, and collaboratively selected a path that led to a happy ending where she married Hamlet.'[57]

The value of relationships

As part of its business strategy, Amazon has seen the need to acquire customers, not simply sell products. Once you have customers, you can sell them a host of different products, not just books, and also services – such as Amazon Prime, their membership service which offers free delivery and other benefits such as ebook lending. You can personalize their shopping experience with customized web pages and emailed special offers.

Traditionally publishers, and to a great extent bookstores, did not know who their customers were to any level of detail. They had some research about the market as a whole, and their own intuitions as to what would or would not sell, but no hard data. The supplier/customer relationships which had value were instead between the author and the publisher, and the publisher and the bookseller. John Thompson, in his book *Merchants of Culture*, views publishers as having five key resources:

> Economic capital is the accumulated financial resources, including stock and plant as well as capital reserves, to which publishers have access, either directly (in their own accounts) or indirectly (through their ability to draw on the resources of a parent company or raise finance from banks or other institutions). Human capital is the staff employed by the firm and their accumulated knowledge, skills and experience. Social capital is the networks of contacts and relationships that an individual or organization has built up over time. Intellectual capital (or intellectual property) consists in the rights that a publisher owns or controls in intellectual content, rights that are attested to by their stock of contracts with authors and other bodies and that they are able to exploit through their publications and through the selling of subsidiary rights. Symbolic capital is the accumulated prestige and status associated with the publishing house.[58]

Economic and symbolic capital are particularly important for determining the competitive position of the firm. In the area of social capital, Thompson details relationships with agents, suppliers, and retailers. Symbolic capital may hold sway with authors and some readers, as well as with key intermediaries such as booksellers and reviewers. Authors may build up their own symbolic capital, becoming brands in their own right.

Let us look in more detail at the area of intellectual capital. Intangible assets – for example copyrights, brands, customer relationships – make up most of the value held in a publishing company, adding up to their intellectual capital. This value can only be fully reflected in a balance sheet once a company is purchased, due to accounting rules.[59] The value held in stock, by contrast, although presented in the

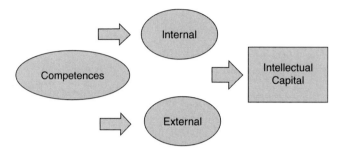

FIGURE 4.1 Knowledge-based strategy. Based on Sveiby (2001)

balance sheet, is difficult to assess since some of it may be unsaleable. Also the notion starts to lose meaning when we think about ebooks and other digital products. Essentially publishers create value by transferring and converting the knowledge held in and by their companies – publishing is part of the knowledge economy.

A publisher uses the *competences* of its staff to create *internal* value, for example creating and spreading best practice through the company and encouraging innovation. Value is created *externally* through its work with authors, which is then converted into copyrights, licences, and trade marks.[60] Value created through working with customers is reflected in the brand of the publisher's lists or of its authors. Mostly publishers have worked with key account customers – bookshop chains, supermarkets, and so on – rather than directly with consumers. There are exceptions when strong publishing brands are created, such as the Dummies range of titles. What digital disruption has done is to threaten the value in the relationships with, say, high street bookshops, and expose the publishers to the fact that they don't have relationships with the end consumers. Certainly they can work with intermediaries in the case of ebooks, but it is primarily a retailer such as Amazon who holds the value of the relationship with the consumer. Amazon, by setting up working relationships with authors, is also further threatening the value created by publishers. Publishers who have worked hard to develop author brands, which create backlist sales, may find those brands lured away by the prospect of self-publishing or working more directly with Amazon. Authors with strong brands can own the relationships with their readers, and will question what level of service they are receiving from publishers. Defending the system of copyright is no longer the key issue in a world where value is being dissipated around you. The necessity is to develop a direct relationship with your customers, and to use digital tools to create *digital capital*.

Amazon has been expert in building value through a process of co-creation with its customers, who play an active role in how the company creates and competes for value. The collective knowledge of the customer base is adding value to the business.[61] Customer reviews and ratings contribute to the quality of the service they receive, alongside recommendations which derive from their own purchasing and browsing history. The company is also using this approach with authors, who can self-publish with Amazon and get real-time data on their sales. Contrast this with a publisher which might only issue sales summaries twice a year.

A network model and digital capital

The old, linear publishing model is now outmoded in an environment where authors can talk to each other, readers can join together in communities, and authors can talk direct to their readership and receive feedback on their work. Social media tools enable low-cost interactions and new types of conversation, alongside face-to-face interactions where possible, for example at events or in reading groups. The issue for publishers is whether they are part of the communities which develop, in a network model, or will simply become bypassed.[62] They need to generate a new kind of capital – digital capital – which encompasses an interaction with consumers, who participate in a conversation and a community, facilitated by digital tools, around authorship, readership, and the co-creation of value.[63] The key questions companies must address are as follows. Which, or whose, brands work best in an online world? Can they develop a community around their content, rather than be left out of the conversation? Are there ways to involve authors and readers in product development? For example, readers may suggest new titles and authors, and offer feedback on projects in development.[64]

In the digital world, the focus has shifted from individual products to providing a service, and towards building a relationship with the end consumer. Those in the middle run the risk of disintermediation – being left out of the value chain – unless

FIGURE 4.2 Linear model

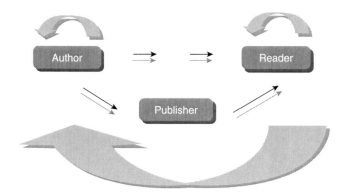

FIGURE 4.3 Network model with feedback

they can develop digital capital and develop their brand so that it works well with consumers. Do books need publishers, or even agents in this new order? Physical booksellers offer one solution to the issue of discoverability, but without an online presence their days are numbered, and publishers have to prepare for a world without this channel to market. As Mike Shatzkin says, 'The book publishers' central competence, which their entire business is built around, is "We put books on shelves" ... if there are no shop windows, then what is the publishers' contribution exactly? It is a really existentialist question.'[65] Even if discoverability is not perceived as a problem by book consumers, who may have their own strategies for finding a title to read, it is a large headache for publishers if they cannot guarantee some visibility for titles in which they have invested both time and money. Already successful authors, who have the brand and the relationships with their readers, may possess considerable digital capital – they have readers following them on their website, blog, and social media. This puts them in a strong position to negotiate better terms with publishers, partner in new ways, or go direct to their readers. The case may be different for a new author, who still requires editorial and marketing effort for them to find an audience (unless they are manic at self-promotion), and it appears to be harder for non-fiction authors to build credibility online.

In the area of romance, Harlequin, Mills & Boon has cracked the issue of how to build a direct relationship with their consumers. They issue new titles on a regular basis and sell ebooks direct from their own digital platform at the same price as their paperbacks. Ebooks work well for romance titles as they offer instant availability to readers with often high rates of consumption – you can start the next title straight away – and the element of privacy about reading and purchasing habits: 'No longer are they forced to conceal the covers of their latest purchases

FIGURE 4.4 Digital capital

(*The Sultan's Choice*, say, or *The Temp and the Tycoon*) from fellow commuters. Instead, they can follow their heroine's romantic adventures with impunity, safely protected by the anonymity of their e-readers.'[66] A survey carried out by the company amongst its readers in 2010 revealed that 44 per cent were purchasing their ebooks direct from the Harlequin website.[67]

Mike Shatzkin has propounded the idea of verticals. Publishers should move away from trying to publish everything towards concentrating on niches. They can then enter into a direct relationship with their customers, and find out what they would like to read. This community of readers can suggest new titles, feedback on works in progress, and will then have a high level of involvement. 'Essentially the concept is that publishers have to talk directly to their audiences. You cannot talk directly to your audiences unless you have consistent content over time. That means you can't do everything; you have to pick your audiences. ... It is audience-centric rather than product-centric.'[68] A number of verticals within the same company can share a common infrastructure, allowing the publisher to reach narrower and smaller niches alongside the larger opportunities.

Some publishers have already made the transition to building a direct relationship with their readers, and ebooks enable them to sell direct with some ease. Or else they may offer a service to brand authors, helping to manage the relationship with readers. But the challenges are significant in a faster, more connected world, where symbolic capital built up in the offline world may count for nothing. There are also new opportunities which arise from such an environment, as we shall see in the next chapter, with the potential for digital content to reach right around the world.

Notes

1 John Markoff, 'The Passion of Steve Jobs', *New York Times*, 15 January 2008.
2 Quoted in Jeffrey Toobin, 'Google's Moon Shot: The quest for the universal library', *New Yorker*, 5 February 2007.
3 Brian Morrissey, 'Marketer of the Year: Jeff Bezos', *Media Week*, 14 September 2009, page 30.
4 PWC report, *Understanding how US online shoppers are reshaping the retail experience*, 2012.
5 Ibid., page 6.
6 Ibid., page 12.
7 Clayton M. Christensen, *The Innovator's Dilemma: When new technologies cause great firms to fail*, Harvard Business School Press, 1997, page 84.
8 Ibid., page 226. In *The Everything Store: Jeff Bezos and the age of Amazon* (Little Brown, 2013), Brad Stone reveals that in 2004 Jeff Bezos started a secret new hardware project at 'Lab126': 'they were to disrupt Amazon's own successful bookselling business with an e-book device' (ebook, loc 3417 of 6180).
9 Interviewed by the author, 13 March 2013.
10 Julie Bosman, 'The Bookstore's Last Stand', *New York Times*, 28 January 2012; Yvonne Zipp, 'The Novel Resurgence of Independent Bookstores', *Christian Science Monitor*, 17 March 2013.
11 Quoted in chapter 8, 'Mr Dunlop and the Blow-up Doll', of Graham Jones, *Last Shop Standing: Whatever happened to record shops*, Omnibus Press, 2010. The ebook consulted had no page numbers. The book is full of wonderful anecdotes, including the woman who brought back her CD single by Kenny the Kangaroo, complaining that it jumped.

96 Digital capital

12 In the UK: 'Bookshops are also a vital cog in the discovery process. They account for 45% of spending on books where the buyer hadn't yet decided what book it is they want to buy.' Jo Henry, 'Discovery Channel', *Bookseller* blog, http://www.thebookseller.com/blogs/discovery-channel.html, accessed 6 May 2013.

13 Jim Milliot, 'Acting on Impulse', *Publishers Weekly*, 23 May 2011.

14 Laura Hazard Owen, 'Why Online Book Discovery Is Broken (and How to Fix it)', paidContent, http://paidcontent.org/2013/01/17/why-online-book-discovery-is-broken-and-how-to-fix-it/, accessed 19 February 2013.

15 David Streitfeld, 'App Writers Find Riches Are Elusive', *New York Times International Weekly*, 25 November 2012.

16 Barry Schwartz, *The Paradox of Choice: Why more is less*, HarperCollins, 2004, ebook, page 140 of 278.

17 Mike Spies, 'Spotify and its Discontents', *New Yorker* blog, http://www.newyorker.com/online/blogs/culture/2012/11/spotify-and-its-discontents.html#ixzz2CC8oL1kF, accessed 14 November 2012.

18 Angus Phillips, 'How Books are Positioned in the Market: Reading the cover', in Nicole Matthews and Nickianne Moody, *Judging a Book by its Cover: Fans, publishers, designers and the marketing of fiction*, Ashgate, 2007, page 28.

19 Interviewed by the author, 13 March 2013.

20 Interviewed by the author, 20 December 2012. This activity is called showrooming.

21 Chad W. Post, *The Three Per Cent Problem: Rants and responses on publishing, translation, and the future of reading*, Open Letter, 2011, chapter X, 'The Age of Screens', ebook, 94% through.

22 Nielsen, *State of the Media: Consumer usage report*, 2011, page 7. Available at http://www.nielsen.com/content/dam/corporate/us/en/reports-downloads/2011-Reports/StateofMediaConsumerUsageReport.pdf, accessed 19 October 2012.

23 See http://www.goodreads.com/about/us, accessed 20 May 2013.

24 Judith A. Chevalier and Dina Mayzlin, 'The Effect of Word of Mouth on Sales: Online book reviews', *Journal of Marketing Research*, 43 (2006), August, page 349.

25 Laura Roberts, 'Award-winning Historian Orlando Figes: I posted anonymous reviews on Amazon', *Daily Telegraph*, 24 April 2010.

26 David Streitfeld, 'The Best Book Reviews Money Can Buy', *New York Times*, 25 August 2012.

27 Cheng-Hsi Fang, Tom M. Y. Lin, Fangyi Liu, and Yu Hsiang Lin, 'Product Type and Word of Mouth: A dyadic perspective', *Journal of Research in Interactive Marketing*, 5:2 (2011), page 197.

28 Jo Brown, Amanda J. Broderick, and Nick Lee, 'Word of Mouth Communication within Online Communities: Conceptualizing the online social network', *Journal Of Interactive Marketing*, 21:3 (2007), Summer, page 15.

29 As mentioned earlier, the website Goodreads was purchased by Amazon in 2013.

30 Killian Fox, 'Laurent Binet: Most French writers are lazy', *Guardian*, 27 April 2012.

31 Ibid., page 16.

32 Yun Kuei Huang and Wen I. Yang, 'Dissemination Motives and Effects of Internet Book Reviews', *The Electronic Library*, 28:6 (2010), page 813.

33 Figures supplied by the book's agent in China, Jackie Huang of Andrew Nurnberg Associates, Beijing. Interviewed by the author, 15 January 2013.

34 The full list of engines which generate conversational capital: Rituals, Exclusive Product Offering, Myths, Relevant Sensory Oddity, Icons, Tribalism, Endorsement, and Continuity. Bertrand Cesvet (with Tony Babinski and Eric Alper), *Conversational Capital: How to create stuff people love to talk about*, FT Press, 2009.

35 Walter Isaacson, *Steve Jobs*, Hachette Digital, 2011, ebook, page 775 of 906.

36 British Council website, http://literature.britishcouncil.org/zadie-smith, accessed 25 July 2012.

37 Derek Larsen and John J. Watson, 'A Guide Map to the Terrain of Gift Value', *Psychology and Marketing*, 18:8 (2001), August, page 893.

38 Ibid., page 894.

39 Liz Macdonald, *A New Chapter: Public library services in the 21st century*, Carnegie Trust, May 2012, page 30.

40 Robert Putnam, 'Social capital: Measurement and consequences', *Canadian Journal of Policy Research*, 2 (2001), pages 41–51.

41 Text sourced from http://www.mimoa.eu/projects/United%20Kingdom/London/Idea%20Store, accessed 20 May 2013.

42 Catherine A. Johnson, 'How Do Public Libraries Create Social Capital? An analysis of interactions between library staff and patrons', *Library & Information Science Research*, 34 (2012), page 56.

43 Miguel Bustillo, 'Library that Holds no Books', *Wall Street Journal*, 6 February 2013.

44 Interviewed by Matthew Cain for C4 News in the UK. Available at http://blogs.channel4.com/culture/downloaded-ebooks-saviour-libraries/3301, accessed 26 September 2012.

45 Benedicte Page and Helen Pidd, 'Ebook restrictions leave libraries facing virtual lockout', *Guardian*, 26 October 2010.

46 William Sieghart, *An Independent Review of E-Lending in Public Libraries in England*, report for the Department of Culture, Media and Sport, March 2013. Available at https://www.gov.uk/government/publications/an-independent-review-of-e-lending-in-public-libraries-in-england, accessed 23 September 2013.

47 Interviewed by the author, 19 November 2012.

48 Nielsen, op. cit., page 7.

49 Ibid., page 6.

50 Ilias Leontiadis, Christos Efstratiou, Marco Picone, and Cecilia Mascolo, 'Don't Kill My Ads! Balancing privacy in an ad-supported mobile application market', *HotMobile*, 12 (2012), 28–9 February.

51 Sarah E. Needleman and Angus Loten, 'When Freemium fails', *Wall Street Journal*, 22 August 2012.

52 Fu Chenzhou of China Mobile, interviewed by the author, 11 January 2013. See also Xiang Ren and Lucy Montgomery, 'Chinese Online Literature: Creative consumers and evolving business models', *Arts Marketing*, 2:2 (2012), pages 118–30.

53 Yahoo, United States Patent Application, No. 20120084136, 5 April 2012.

54 Martin Arnold, 'Making Books: Placed products, and their cost', *New York Times*, 13 September 2001.

55 Christina Lamb, 'Is Obama Stalking You?', *Spectator*, 27 October 2012, page 17.

56 James Surowiecki, *The Wisdom of the Crowds: Why the many are smarter than the few*, Little, Brown, 2004.

57 Laura Hudson, 'Record-Breaking Kickstarter Turns Hamlet Into a Choose-Your-Adventure Epic', *Wired*, 20 December 2012.

58 John Thompson, *Merchants of Culture: The publishing business in the 21st century*, 2nd edition, Polity Press, 2012, page 6.

59 Usually the difference in value between a company's assets and its purchase value is classified as goodwill – those elements which contribute to its competitive advantage, including its brand and employees.

60 The knowledge-based strategy was first presented here: Angus Phillips, 'The importance of intellectual capital in book publishing', Fifth International Conference on Information Law and Ethics, Ionian Academy, Corfu, Greece, 29 June 2012. This is based on the approach taken by Karl-Erik Sveiby in his article 'A Knowledge-Based Theory of the Firm to Guide in Strategy Formulation', *Journal of Intellectual Capital*, 2:4 (2001), pages 344–58.

61 C. K. Prahalad and Venkatram Ramaswamy, 'Co-Opting Customer Competence', *Harvard Business Review* (2000), January, pages 79–87.

62 The network model was first presented here: Angus Phillips, 'Epublishers: From theory to practice', III Foro Internacional de Edicion Universitaria, Feria Internacional del Libro, Guadalajara, Mexico, December 2008.

98 Digital capital

63 The term digital capital was used by Don Tapscott, David Ticoll, and Alex Lowy, for their book on building wealth through business webs or b-webs: *Digital Capital: Harnessing the Power of Business Webs*, Harvard Business School Press, 2000.

64 As an example of co-creation offline, the UK publisher And Other Stories has as one of its commandments that 'Names of authors or books generating excitement in reading groups (not necessarily unanimous) should be suggested to the core team for inclusion in the next acquisitions meeting.' See http://www.andotherstories.org/about/11-commandments/, accessed 6 May 2013.

65 Interviewed by the author, 13 March 2013.

66 Alison Flood, 'Romantic Fiction's Passion for Ebooks', *Guardian*, 10 October 2011.

67 Association of Learned and Professional Society Publishers, *E-Book Strategies The essential ALPSP guide on how to develop your e-book offer*, 2011, page 83.

68 Interviewed by the author, 13 March 2013. He cites Osprey in the UK and F+W Media in the USA as two key examples of this approach.

5

THE GLOBAL BOOK

Publishers are repositioning themselves to take advantage of the globalization of book markets. They are reviewing their internal structures and are keen to obtain the world rights to potential bestsellers. The success of authors such as Stephanie Meyer and Stieg Larsson has shown how books can sell in large numbers across a variety of markets, and franchises can develop in other media. Will the growth of ebooks drive the penetration of bestsellers across different markets? What will happen in smaller markets, faced with competition from the global players?

For books two key trends are driving globalization: digitization and the growth of reading in English around the world. A bestselling author has the opportunity to see revenues from rights deals in other languages, and from export editions in the original language. With the global reach of ebooks, the original language edition can be accessed directly by a consumer. If the printing press enabled scalability, so that one book can reach many different readers, then the ebook is even more scalable in that demand can be satisfied straight away almost anywhere in the world.

Towards a global culture?

Globalization is one of the key trends of the late twentieth and early twenty-first centuries. You can walk down a street in Istanbul or Shanghai and discover a McDonald's or a Starbucks. Fashion and luxury brands have a global reach and a global appeal, leading to a homogenization of tastes which dampens local and cultural differences. Film franchises, such as Twilight and the Bond movies, are developed with a global audience in mind. This leads to higher box office sales and the opportunity to raise revenues from product placement. The internet offers content, games, memes, photos, and videos which can be accessed all over the world.

There is a dualist concept of globalization which recognizes the need for local cultures and ethnic groups to express their identities whilst acknowledging the homogenization of tastes around global brands. Globalization makes the world smaller and more connected, and unleashes social, economic, and technological impacts on a much bigger scale; at the same time it diminishes the powers of national governments and encourages the revival of regional or local identities. Localism in Scotland or Catalonia is partly a response to the forces of globalization. The anthropologist Jonathan Friedman wrote in 1990: 'Ethnic and cultural fragmentation and modernist homogenization are not two arguments, two opposing views of what is happening in the world today, but two constitutive trends of global reality.'[1]

Whilst consumer companies see the potential for expansion in new markets around the world, they also recognize the need to adapt to local tastes and the needs of new markets. In the twenty-first century, globalization is not necessarily Westernization. Rian Johnson, the director of the film *Looper*, which premiered in 2012, said that he was happy to change the location of the movie from Paris to Shanghai to benefit from Chinese funding and increase the likelihood of box office success in the Chinese market. This reflects the fact that China is now the largest foreign market for Hollywood films.[2]

A global world generates global phenomena, and sometimes from surprising directions. In 2012 a pop song which came from nowhere to become a major viral hit was 'Gangnam Style' by the South Korean star Psy. Not especially notable for its music, the pop video launched a new dance craze and became the most liked entry ever on YouTube. In just two months the video was viewed over 200m times and by the end of the year it had received an astonishing 1bn views.[3]

In previous chapters we have seen the effects of digitization on the media industries, opening up a global audience. When in 2012 the 25 billionth app was downloaded from the Apple store, the app was 'Where's My Water?', and the consumer was in Qingdao in China. This Disney game is a 'fun, simple – yet challenging – physics-based puzzle game featuring Swampy the Alligator and his quest to take a shower'.[4] Launched in 2011, in its first year the game reached the number one spot in a whole range of countries, and was downloaded over one hundred million times.

Just as games have a global audience, so do some newspapers through their websites, and among the most popular are *The New York Times* and the Mail Online (*Daily Mail*) from the UK. *Der Spiegel* from Germany reaches a global market with an English language edition. With their digital presence some papers have found that half their readership comes from outside their home countries. Now that three-quarters of the world's population has access to a mobile phone, the opportunities to produce content for a world market are larger than ever before.[5] Around a quarter of mobile devices are used to access the internet, and the developing world has followed a different path to the developed world with what is called the 'mobile first' trajectory of communications. Users will often have a cell phone before they have computer access; and these countries have pioneered micro-payments using mobile phones. Low-priced tablets, in all markets, are set to revolutionize access to the internet and a range of content including ebooks. In a region such as the Arab world, where the distribution network for physical books is poor, ebooks can reach all parts of the market. In Brazil there are fewer than 1,000 bookshops for a population of nearly 200m people, and there are large parts of the north of the country with little access to physical books. The Brazilian journalist and publisher Carlo Carrenho says that 'digital brings this huge revolution in distribution and access for the people of Brazil'.[6] The effects will only be amplified by ongoing experiments in the area of education, where digital developments proceed apace: for example the Fatih project in Turkey aims to equip all teachers and students with tablet computers, with 16m being given out over a period of four years.[7]

The TV market has become truly global and we are familiar with the dominance of US shows around the world, either dubbed or shown with subtitles. In recent years there has been the growth of format television – branded formats sold into a number of countries. For example, reality or talent shows originating in one country are then sold around the world. A prominent example is the *Big Brother* format, which first aired in the Netherlands in 1999: by the mid-2000s 30 licences had been sold to other countries by the production company Endemol. Similarly *Pop Idol* was first shown in the UK in 2001, and by 2008 over 40 licences had been sold, covering over 50 different territories. The US version of the show, *American Idol*, was in turn sold to over 180 countries, proving that both the format and a local version would travel.[8] Why did the format market take off so rapidly, having grown very slowly for a number of years? Jean Chalaby argues this is the result of a combination of factors, including the growth in domestic television around the world, and the need for more local content. The shows come with some guarantee of success behind them, which lowers risk, and the format shows can be adapted locally to suit the needs of a domestic audience. There has also been the growth of independent production, in particular in Europe, which has encouraged innovation and creativity. This has been notable in the UK, where producers can hold on to a range of rights when they sell a show to a TV channel. This enables them to exploit the international market.[9]

Research into the influence of American popular culture shows its growing power internationally, and to a mostly receptive, rather than resistant audience. Between 2007 and 2012 there was generally increasing enthusiasm for US music, movies, and TV shows around the world. In Europe there was particular enthusiasm, with up to 90 per cent of 18- to 29-year-olds liking US culture in many countries (Germany 94 per cent, Italy 88 per cent, and Poland 79 per cent). The figures were lower in other parts of the world: China 56 per cent; India 24 per cent; and Pakistan 10 per cent. The last figure is understandable given the context of the unpopularity of the USA's political and military actions. By contrast when the US population was asked whether they like music, movies, and television from other countries, 53% said they do, while 39% responded that they do not.[10]

102 The global book

There is a whole debate about the diminishing of local culture in the face of what can be seen as cultural imperialism, and John Tomlinson has two reflections on the significance of the spread of Western media. Firstly the influence of media should be seen as part of a whole set of other changes in people's lives, which he calls the 'impact of capitalist modernity'. These include living in cities, industrialization, and the division of life into separate spheres (work, 'private life'). As their lives change, people come to draw more on media imagery in their constructions of reality. He also points out that the conclusion of empirical studies about the viewing of television, for example, shows that audiences are more active and critical, more reflective, and more resistant to manipulation than many theorists have supposed.[11]

For the book market there has always been the opportunity to publish for a global market, either in original editions or locally adapted titles (this would include both direct translation and adaptation of the text and illustrations). This of course depends on the particular book and its suitability, and many titles would only have a local appeal, but the global success of, say, the biography of Steve Jobs by Walter Isaacson shows the potential upside. Delivery of a printed book to another market might take several weeks, and ebooks offer the advantage for the consumer of instant delivery. There are some markets in which editions compete with each other, and custom and practice usually favour particular originating countries or publishers. Digital publication enables greater competition and will lead to lower prices for some titles. The growth of global culture, in particular in the youth market, offers opportunities for books to join other media in having blockbuster potential. Nassim Nicholas Taleb argues that the success of movies and other cultural products depends on contagions. 'It is hard for us to accept that people do not fall in love with works of art only for their own sake, but also in order to feel that they belong to a community. By imitating, we get closer to others – that is, other imitators.'[12] New devices and platforms encourage the convergence of media, which helps books to merge with other media in the mind of the consumer. A good example of this is the phenomenal success of the Hunger Games franchise. As the industry analyst Rüdiger Wischenbart says: 'books suddenly merge into that pop culture and pop youth culture, and merge into other media such as pop music and a certain type of movies.'[13] The growth of ebooks offers the prospect of even greater rewards and the opportunity to penetrate markets more directly. In particular this offers potential for books in the English language.

Lingua franca

David Crystal divides the speakers of English into three categories: native speakers, speakers of English as a second language, and learners of English as a foreign language. India, Singapore, and Malawi are examples of countries where English plays an important role as the second language amongst a multilingual setting. Overall, including learners of English as a foreign language, the total number of English speakers was estimated at one-quarter of the world's population at the beginning of the twenty-first century. 'In 1950, the case for English as a world language would have been no more than plausible. Fifty years on, and the case is virtually unassailable.'[14] Since the beginning of the twenty-first century, the world's population has expanded by a further billion, but also the number of English learners has expanded, with for example some estimates suggesting that 300m people are learning English in China (a quarter of its population).[15]

What this is doing to the language itself is the subject of much discussion, with the growth of more fragmented dialects – 'Englishes' – around the world. Alongside there is a more standardized and simplified form of English, sometimes called Globish – English as a lingua franca. This is the dominant language of communication in the world of global business, and a knowledge of the language is an essential skill for those working internationally. It is also the language of the web, and it is estimated that over 80 per cent of the home pages on the internet are available in English.[16]

Taking the European market for books, there is a healthy market for books in English. Miha Kovač believes that the levels of penetration are higher in those smaller countries where translations may appear more slowly and at the same time the population has good linguistic skills in English. He estimates that on average sales are between 5 and 10 per cent of total sales in such countries as Denmark and Norway, reaching as high as 15 per cent in Slovenia. Sales of *Fifty Shades of Grey*, a bestseller in Slovenia, dropped by 80 per cent once the local translation became available.[17] The novelist Tim Parks, who lives in Italy, comments on the reading both of English books and of translations from English around Europe:

> The surprise is that increased knowledge of English has also brought a much more marked increase in sales of literature written in English but read in translation in the local language. When you learn a language you don't just pick up a means of communication, you buy into a culture, you get interested.[18]

In his research into readers in the Netherlands, he found quite startling reasons for choosing translations of English novels over Dutch fiction. Some respondents said the books were better; others that they wanted to read books they could talk about when they travelled: 'Nobody outside Holland knows Dutch novels. It's good to know the big book of the moment, Franzen, Rushdie, what everybody's talking about.' Alongside the prevalence of a popular culture which crosses frontiers and media, we also have the rise of literary authors attracting an international audience. With the global dominance of the English language, and now translations from English, an unfair advantage has developed, with a momentum of its own, regardless of the quality of the books. This also has implications for authorship, with some authors choosing to write for an international readership, with a consequent shift in content and style. Parks says this development may be conscious or

104 The global book

not. In China, according to the publisher Fangzhou Yang, the typical reader of translated fiction is likely to be a white collar professional, perhaps female and 'between 18 and 40 years old, typically the rising middle class, who has a yearning for a more Western life style (drinking coffee, going on vacations, etc.) and who is quite well off to afford books of good qualities'.[19]

Writing from a Lithuanian viewpoint, Milda Danyté comments on the dominance of English authors in the global market for teen fiction:

> Although it is theoretically possible that some Dane, Lithuanian, Czech or Bulgarian writer could produce the next global bestseller for youth, it is very unlikely because English-language publishers are wary of translated texts, and it is only the very largest of these publishers who can afford to invest in the kind of campaign that makes a book a global success.[20]

From this perspective the success of Stieg Larsson in crime fiction, for example, is seen as an exception to the general picture.

We can see elsewhere in the world the development of writing for a more global audience. Prominence has been given to Indian authors writing literary fiction in English, including Salman Rushdie, Amitav Ghosh, Vikram Seth, Arundhati Roy, Rohinton Mistry, and Anita Desai. The latter recalls that for her first book she was taken on by a small independent publishing house in London, the reason being that no Indian publisher was interested in publishing fiction by a local author.

> There was, in those years, an antipathy, a hostility even, towards writing in English – the colonial language that should have been banned outright at independence. I tried to ignore the assumption that mine was the last generation in India that would write in English but shared in the sense that these were its twilight years. The picture changed abruptly, dramatically, in 1981, when a book called *Midnight's Children* appeared like a thunderbolt and the author was sent to India on that until then unknown exercise, a book tour.[21]

The international success of Salman Rushdie transformed perceptions of what was possible for Indian authors writing in English, and in the late 1990s the London literary agent David Godwin took the unusual step of flying to India to sign up Arundhati Roy, whose *The God of Small Things* went on to win the Booker in 1997. It was now possible for Indian English to shine as a medium, taking on Indian subjects and themes. This has extended to a burgeoning market for commercial fiction written in English, and according to Suman Gupta, authors can 'embody their Indian identities over their regional identities by dint of writing in English'.[22]

Taking another example, there have been significant efforts to ensure that Korean authors are translated in Western markets. Financial support for translations has been forthcoming from the Korean Literature Translation Institute and the Daesan Foundation, which have been keen to promote Korean literature in international markets. There have been some breakthroughs, and the success of *Please Look after Mum* (2009) by Kyung-sook Shin, which sold in 35 countries and won the Man Asian Literary Prize, has helped to stimulate interest in Korean writing. The tale is of an elderly woman from the countryside who travels to Seoul to visit her adult children and then gets lost in a scramble to get on the subway in Seoul. Shin's agent Barbara J. Zitwer, who represents a number of Korean authors, says: '[Her] book paved the way for everyone else and opened doors.'[23]

Reflecting on the issues around the translation of Korean literature, An Sonjae, who has worked on many texts published in English, identifies some key problems including the contrasting language systems and the cultural and historical assumptions inherent in Korean literature. Some regard the literature as quite depressing, and he acknowledges that many of the short stories and novels enjoyed by Koreans make harrowing reading. The events of Korean history are so familiar to domestic readers that they are often evoked by a string of numbers or a single name: for example 1026 refers to the assassination on 26 October 1979 of President Park Chung-hee by the head of his security service.

> The problem facing the translator here is probably insoluble. Since the Korean readership brings intense emotional associations ready-made to the least mention of these and a host of similar moments, Korean writers feel no need to explain background or even make very explicit the events they are referring to. Footnotes will never provide enough information to awaken the same feelings in a non-Korean.[24]

Barbara J. Zitwer comes to the defence of the style of Korean fiction: 'I think readers today want books of substance and Korean writers are dealing with many issues that are relevant to the world – there is nothing superficial about the writing – and that is refreshing compared to all the vampire and sex books popular in the west.'[25] Compare this to the experience of a third-generation Korean American, the writer Don Lee, who has enjoyed critical and commercial success with his novels and short stories. He became concerned about the perils of being pigeon-holed as writing Asian American literature:

> In the end, I couldn't stop my book from being ghettoized as ethnic lit, I couldn't stop those cute little references in reviews to geishas and fortune cookies and kimchee. In the end, I managed to piss off pretty much everyone – either for being too Asian, or not Asian enough.[26]

Casey Brienza, who has examined the introduction of manga into the USA, expresses frustration at what she calls the tragedy of globalization. As manga was incorporated into the mainstream in America, and attracted the attention of the larger publishing groups, it detached itself from its Japanese context and culture.

106 The global book

Instead it came to represent a comic book published in a certain trim size, or alternatively a category of comics read by girls and women, and in the end 'just another category of books, like cookbooks, science fiction, or biographies'. Whilst its content retains some 'Japaneseness', manga in the end did not make the Americans more Japanese.[27]

Homogenization and translation

What evidence is there already of a homogenization of tastes around the reading of books? Studies of bestseller lists in Europe by Miha Kovač and Rüdiger Wischenbart have showed a reasonable level of diversity.[28] Overall the majority of bestsellers were either written in local languages or translated from the larger languages of English, French, German, and Spanish (a notable exception was Swedish). In their research they developed an impact factor for authors, showing that for western Europe, in the period 2008–9, 19 out of the 40 authors with the highest impact factor were writing in English, and 21 in other languages. An examination of book markets in eastern Europe revealed that of the 40 authors with the highest impact factors, 13 were writing in English, 10 in other languages, and a further 17 were domestic authors. A startling finding was that no work originally written in an eastern European language could be spotted on the western European bestseller lists; in addition no domestic bestseller in an eastern European country had transferred to other markets in that region. This does suggest a one-way street in favour of the larger languages. This is confirmed by a 2006 study of 15,000 translations appearing in the Serbian language, which discovered that 74 per cent were from English, 8 per cent from French, and 6 per cent from German, leaving only small percentages to Polish, Slovenian, and Bulgarian.[29] In the Netherlands, three out of four translations are from English; and only 10 per cent of all translations are from languages other than English, French, and German.[30]

Digging deeper into the statistics does start to tease out more diversity. For example, although the percentage of translations from other languages has remained stable in the Netherlands, the range of languages has become broader compared to the 1980s.[31] If we turn to France, whilst there is a low level of diversity in the area of bestsellers, the picture changes with the examination of literary fiction. For example, amongst one series of bestsellers (crime, thrillers, and science fiction), three-quarters of the books were translated from English, and one-quarter were titles written in French. By contrast for series of literary fiction, of the titles analysed in one study, only between one-quarter and one-third were translated from English, with works translated from up to 36 languages.[32] Gisèle Sapiro writes that 'With regards to linguistic and geographic origins of translations, the opposition between homogenization and diversity thus coincides with the opposition between commercial and upmarket.'[33]

In the Brazilian market there is a contrasting picture between non-fiction and fiction. In non-fiction, local authors dominate and in recent years there have been a number of successful narrative titles, for example about the history of Brazil.

Examination of sales data over a two-year period (2011–12) shows how for the top 20 selling non-fiction titles, 16 were by domestic authors, and their books sold 81 per cent of the total number of copies. In the area of fiction, however, the best-seller lists were dominated by commercial fiction translated from English. Out of the top 20 titles, 18 were translations and just two by Brazilian writers, Fábio de Melo and Jô Soares; and of those 18, just one title (by Umberto Eco), was not translated from English. Of the total copies sold of the top 20 titles, 88 per cent were of the translated titles from English.[34]

Clear across a number of markets is the dominance of English, especially in commercial fiction, and the benefits for writers who can write for an international market. The 'translation gap' has been well documented and figures on translations from UNESCO's Index Translationum show the imbalance of translations from and to English. Table 5.1 shows the top ten languages from which translations have been made; the database was started in 1979. Table 5.2 shows the target languages

TABLE 5.1 Top ten languages from which translations have been made since 1979

	Original language	Number of translations
1	English	1,226,389
2	French	217,841
3	German	201,193
4	Russian	101,771
5	Italian	66,697
6	Spanish	52,872
7	Swedish	39,149
8	Japanese	27,014
9	Danish	20,892
10	Latin	19,321

TABLE 5.2 Target languages for translations since 1979

	Target language	Number of translations
1	German	290,918
2	French	239,655
3	Spanish	228,272
4	English	153,433
5	Japanese	130,625
6	Dutch	111,242
7	Russian	83,278
8	Polish	76,616
9	Portuguese	74,705
10	Swedish	71,107

Source: Index Translationum, September 2012. The database can be interrogated for the most up-to-date figures: http://portal.unesco.org/culture/en/ev.php-URL_ID=7810&URL_DO=DO_TOPIC&URL_SECTION=201.html

for translations over the same period. Around eight times more titles were translated from English compared to the other way round. By comparison the totals were far more equal for French, German, and Russian. The most translated author, by a considerable distance, is the English author Agatha Christie.

Johan Heilbron argues for a core–periphery view in order to model the languages originating translations, in which English occupies a hyper-central position, with over 50 per cent of translations. Next there are two languages, French and German, with a central position, followed by around seven or eight languages (for example Spanish, Italian, and Russian) with a semi-central position. After this there are all the other languages, with only about 1 per cent of book translations. 'These languages can be considered to be "peripheral" in the international translation economy, in spite of the fact that some of these languages have a very large number of speakers – Chinese, Japanese, Arabic.'[35] The logical consequence of such a model is that rates of translation *into* a language will be lower in countries with languages towards the centre, and higher in countries with languages towards the periphery. Further, some authors now write in English rather than their native language, and are then translated into their domestic market. One example is the Slovenian philosopher Slavoj Žižek, who writes in English and is then translated into Slovene.

The website Three Percent, which advances the cause of international literature, takes its name from the 3 per cent of all books published in the USA which are translated works.[36] Chad Post writes about our reasons for wanting to read

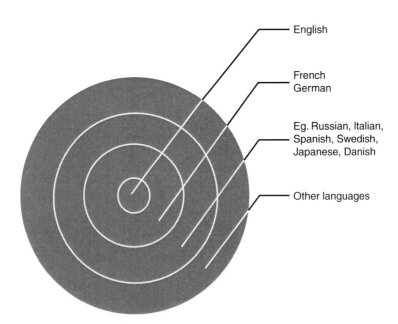

FIGURE 5.1 Core–periphery model

international literature, and perhaps makes some of us feel uncomfortable. He believes that books should stand on their own merits, regardless of their origins:

> One of the reasons that a lot of people give for why they do (or why they should) read international fiction is to 'get a sense of what life is like in other cultures.' Which is sweet and admirable and maybe a bit LolliLove [a mockumentary in which a rich couple try to make a difference by giving the homeless lollipops], but makes a degree of sense. Or does it? Why do we assume that a Japanese writer is going to 'explain' something about Japanese culture?[37]

But if we are going to move away from a Eurocentric view of what is world literature, it is important that we broaden our horizons, whatever the motivation. As people have travelled more, they are more receptive to new cultures and experiences, and there is no reason why they cannot expand their reading to other literatures.

Lawrence Venuti has been highly critical of the trade imbalance in translations, which he believes has serious cultural ramifications. Not only does the imbalance support the expansion of American and British culture, it also promotes a monolingual culture in those countries. In addition readers have become accustomed to fluent translations, which are eminently readable and consumable, to the neglect of texts which might be seen as more difficult. He argues for a higher value to be placed on the work of the translator, to offset their 'invisibility': 'Under the regime of fluent translation, the translator works to make his or her work "invisible," producing the illusory effect of transparency that simultaneously masks its status as an illusion: the translated text seems "natural," that is, not translated.'[38] He maintains that the translator has only a shadowy existence in British and American cultures, and cites how in 1981 John Updike reviewed in the *New Yorker* works by Italo Calvino and Günter Grass with only the barest mention of the translators.

The situation has improved to some extent, and translators such as Anthea Bell are more visible, celebrated and promoted as a selling-point for their translations. But if publishers have found that the best way to push world literature is to present it as mainstream, then highlighting the work as a translation per se could be counterproductive. That Scandinavian crime fiction (and now drama, with the success of *The Killing* a prime example) can be successful on its own merits is a vindication of this strategy. Christopher MacLehose, the publisher who brought Stieg Larsson to the English-speaking world, says that 'A publisher should go where the books are, wherever that may be. The fact that Larsson is in translation has been completely overshadowed in readers' minds by the fact that it is something they want to read. Surely that's as it should be.'[39] Jo Lusby, head of Penguin's office in China, agrees with this approach, talking of their books purchased for translation into English: 'We have approached the books purely from a publishing standpoint, and to look for books that we believe will work.' She bought the English language rights for the Chinese bestseller by Jiang Rong, *Wolf*

Totem (2008), and the book went on to win the first Man Asian Literary Prize and sell hundreds of thousands of copies. She suggests that in order for books to succeed, they first need to work at a local level: 'We all know that books are local, and the success of a book will begin with your next-door neighbour reading a copy, or the postman reading a copy ... Books will always start locally and radiate outwards, always, even with the best marketing campaign.'[40]

Venuti maintains that we should be reading some texts which are difficult, yet research for the Global Translation Initiative into the area of literary translations suggests that their perceived difficulty remains a major obstacle to their success.[41] They suffer from the perception that they are more difficult reads, and therefore hold less potential for popularity. When questioned about likely bias against translations, each part of the book chain looked to other areas. Translators see a bias against translations on the part of publishers, publishers point to a bias in the media, and the media perceives a bias on the part of readers. Yet booksellers, who have the most direct contact with readers, believe that any reader bias against literary translation is minimal.

English has a further role in the world of translations as an intermediary or bridge language between minority languages, alongside the traditional bridge languages of French and German. A detective story can be translated, for example, from Swedish to Hungarian, using the English translation as the mediating text. This reflects a shortage of translators able to work directly between the two languages, and the likelihood that there will be someone available to translate to and from the English. Miha Kovač comments on the situation in Slovenia:

> Translating from English is quite easy. Finding a good translator from Spanish is manageable, and finding a translator from Croatian or from Serbian is also manageable, but for example we had huge problems with Orhan Pamuk. There is only one person who can translate from Turkish to Slovene. So we translate many books from English which are not primarily written in English.[42]

An edition of a book in English also facilitates its transition into a range of other languages in other ways, as Barbara J. Zitwer suggests for Korean titles:

> Selling world English rights helps Korean authors sell in other places because a complete English translation can be commissioned and then shared with others. Many foreign editors do not have Korean readers or translators so they read the English translations and translate from the English rather than directly from the Korean.[43]

Ebooks

With the arrival of ebooks, English language publishers have already seen an uplift in sales of their books in international markets. There is the possibility of reaching all parts of the world, without the need for intermediaries to facilitate the distribution of physical books. A publisher which holds the global rights to a title can offer it as an ebook right around the world, whilst looking to sell rights in local languages. For publishers such as Michael Bhaskar at Profile Books, 'The markets are much more international than they have ever been in the past, so you have to think about books in a global sense, whereas I think previously most publishers around the world thought in a national sense.'[44]

There are some markets where English language books compete directly with local language editions. The Netherlands is a prime example, where a Dutch publisher will aim to have the translated edition available as close as possible to the publication there of the English edition. But a reader may well be tempted to read the book in English if an ebook is readily available at an attractive price. Rüdiger Wischenbart sees price as being influential in markets such as the Netherlands and Scandinavia, where there is already a high level of reading in English:

> In these markets you have such a significant number of people prepared to read in English, that publishers need to consider whether to translate a book from English because the main group of readers may have read that book already. On the one hand it is timing, but it is also pricing. An English language ebook will be available at a very low cost to the local populations everywhere. The local publisher has much higher costs from the translation but also from producing the book in a small print run.[45]

From the viewpoint of Slovenia, Miha Kovač says that 'English books represent competition to Slovenian publishers, and this means that ebooks in English are a very serious problem.'[46]

It is also possible to imagine the translation being commissioned by the originating publisher as part of the original production, if they are willing to extend their financial risk. Just as a film or app can be distributed with a range of language options, an ebook could be made available with a choice of language or suite of languages. At the press of a button you could display a bilingual edition, with text on facing pages. If a publisher wished to produce an ebook in any language requested, what are the prospects for machine translation? Could it be done automatically on request, according to customer preference? At the present time this looks undesirable for fiction, where ease of reading is sought, even should the reader be willing to lose some of the meaning of the original along the way.

For non-fiction, where you might be simply after the information and not the smoothness of the reading experience, there are machine translators that do a pretty good job and may offer 'good enough' content. Most prominently, Google Translate can offer some very good results, because it has the benefit of scanning the web for previous translations of a phrase – often those might have been carried out by a professional translator. This artificial intelligence is based on the crowd-sourcing efforts of many people, and Jaron Lanier bemoans the impact: 'The act of cloud-based translation shrinks the economy by pretending the translators who

112 The global book

provided the examples don't exist. With each so-called automatic translation, the humans who were the sources of the data are inched away from the world of compensation and employment.'[47]

As more machine translations are used, however, the waters are made murkier as Google cannot necessarily discriminate between the sources as to their quality.[48] The Malaysian Ministry of Defence relied on Google Translate to produce English language pages on its website, and the phrase 'pakaian yang menjolok mata', which means 'revealing clothes' in Bahasa Malaysia, was translated as 'clothes that poke eye'.[49]

In his book *The Last Lingua Franca*, Nicholas Ostler describes a study which analysed the outcome of a 12-year project by the European Union to produce a machine translation system amongst the nine languages then used by member states (the report appeared in 1990). It was clear that the project had not produced a functioning system, but even the final report itself had ambiguities. In the French version of the report, the project's work was described as 'insuffisant' (insufficient); in the English version the word used was 'inadequate'.[50] Such nuances highlight the difficulties of perfecting an automated system.

In 2012 Google Translate offered translations between 64 languages, including Latin, Tamil, and Welsh. Again it is only able to do this by relying on the primacy of the English language, and using it as a bridge language. As David Bellos comments:

> The service that Google provides appears to flatten and diversify interlanguage relations beyond the wildest dreams of even the EU's most enthusiastic language parity proponents. But it is able to do so only by exploiting, confirming and increasing the central role played by the most widely translated language in the world's electronic databank of translated texts.[51]

Bellos points out that English-language detective novels may well have been translated into both Icelandic and Farsi, offering the opportunity to find a match between sentences in the two languages. He suggests that the real wizardry of Harry Potter is the way the books enable text to be translated from Hebrew into Chinese. Over time the quality of this method is improving, but even in the medium term there has to remain a place for a human translator who can honour the style and approach of the original author.

Go global

Digital developments offer a broader reach for the book, and can offer new opportunities for authors and publishers, not just from Western markets. In 2011 the Chinese publisher Jiangsu Science and Technology Publishing House produced a book app on acupuncture, sold through the Apple store. There was a relatively modest sale of 1,000 units but 60 per cent of the market was in Europe and North

America. Liu Feng, their Business Development Director, said that 'Digitized books offer an easier way to introduce books overseas compared to the traditional model.'[52] This traditional model would most likely have been selling the print rights in translation to an overseas publisher.

Users can now more directly feed their thoughts into the writing and publication of books, and the same applies in the area of translations. Customer sales and feedback can inform decisions about which titles should be translated, and Amazon has its own imprint, AmazonCrossing, built upon this idea. There are forums to which suggestions can be posted, and the programme's editorial team can spot likely projects through examination of Amazon's own data on sales and customer ratings.

Digital can offer benefits in those countries without a developed infrastructure around the distribution of physical books. A range of content can be accessed directly from domestic publishers, but also from companies operating on a global scale. The tendency towards globalization is a concern for all of those keen to see the preservation of local identities and cultures. The issues are not unique to the book, and many consumers will want to participate in the trends around the latest mobile device, movie, or blockbuster teen fiction. However, the collapse of physical retail for books in some countries, which is being accelerated by the growth of ebooks, and the rise of global bestsellers, are not healthy for the diversity of local book markets. So far the growth of ebooks carries with it benefits for titles in English, which can command a global reach. Whilst it is good for books to be seen as successful, and holding their own against other media, there is the risk of homogenization and little alteration to the imbalance in the flow of translations. The importance remains of interventions to smooth the passage of authors and books between cultures. These include state subsidies for translations and programmes which bring exposure for writers at events or in the media in other countries.

Notes

1 Jonathan Friedman, 'Being in the World: Globalization and localization', in Mike Featherstone (ed.), *Global Culture: Nationalism, Globalization and Modernity*, Sage, 1990, page 311.

2 Helen Pidd, 'Sci-fi Blockbuster Looper Achieves Chinese Box Office First', *Guardian*, 1 October 2012.

3 'PSY's "Gangnam Style" video breaks YouTube's "most liked" record', *NME*, 21 September 2012. Available at http://www.nme.com/news/various-artists/66256, accessed 28 October 2012.

4 See http://disney.go.com/wheresmywater/, accessed 28 September 2012. The year 2012 also saw the 25 billionth Android app sold.

5 The World Bank estimated in 2012 that there were 6bn subscriptions in use worldwide. World Bank, *2012 Information and Communications for Development: Maximizing Mobile*. Available at http://www.worldbank.org/ict/IC4D2012, accessed 23 September 2013.

6 Interviewed by the author, 20 March 2013.

7 See http://fatihproject.com/, accessed 28 September 2012.

8 Jean Chalaby, 'The Making of an Entertainment Revolution: How the TV format trade became a global industry', *European Journal of Communication*, 26:4 (2011).

9 Ibid., pages 304–5.
10 Pew Research Center, Global Attitudes Project, *Global Opinion of Obama Slips, International Policies Faulted*, 13 June 2012.
11 John Tomlinson, *Cultural Imperialism: A critical introduction*, Continuum, 1991, pages 49 and 64.
12 Nassim Nicholas Taleb, *The Black Swan: The impact of the highly improbable*, Penguin, 2007, loc 1010 of 8278 in ebook.
13 Interviewed by the author, 20 December 2012.
14 David Crystal, *English as a Global Language*, 2nd edition, Cambridge University Press, 2003, page 71.
15 See, for example, http://seeingredinchina.com/2011/08/30/is-teaching-english-in-china-a-waste-of-time/, accessed 28 September 2012.
16 Robert McCrum, 'So, what's this Globish Revolution?', *Observer*, 3 December 2006.
17 Interviewed by the author, 23 January 2013.
18 Tim Parks, 'Most Favoured Nations', *New York Review of Books* blog, http://www.nybooks.com/blogs/nyrblog/2012/jun/11/literary-globalization-europe-translation/, accessed 28 September 2012.
19 Fangzhou Yang, Editor at Dook Publishing, interviewed by the author, 8 February 2013.
20 Milda Danyté, 'Translation and Other Transcultural Acts: Resistance to language imperialism in the age of English', page 5, in *Otherness: Essays and Studies 3.1*, edited by Anne Holden Rønning, Centre for Studies in Otherness. Available at http://www.otherness.dk/otherness-essays-studies-3.1/, accessed 5 October 2012.
21 Anita Desai, 'Author author: Aspiring writers from India', *Guardian*, 19 September 2009.
22 Suman Gupta, 'Indian "Commercial" Fiction in English, the Publishing Industry, and Youth Culture', *Economic and Political Weekly*, 46:5 (2012), page 51. See also Vinutha Mallya, 'Dotting the "i" of Indian Publishing', *Logos*, 22:1 (2011).
23 Interviewed by the author, 5 March 2013.
24 An Sonjae, 'Literary Translation from Korean into English: A study in criteria', *Literature and Translation*, 11:1 (2002), page 78.
25 Interviewed by the author, 5 March 2013.
26 Don Lee, 'Uncle Tong: Or, how I learned to speak for all Asian Americans', page 35 in Young-Key Kim-Renaud, R. Richard Grinker, and Kirk W. Larsen, *Korean American Literature*, Sigur Center Asia Papers, 2004. Available at http://www.gwu.edu/~sigur/assets/docs/scap/SCAP20-KoreanWriters.pdf, accessed 20 May 2013.
27 Casey Brienza, 'Books, Not Comics: Publishing fields, globalization, and Japanese manga in the United States', *Publishing Research Quarterly*, 25:2 (2009), page 115.
28 Miha Kovač and Rüdiger Wischenbart, 'A Myth Busted: Bestselling fiction in Europe and Slovenia', *Primerjalna književnost*, Ljubljana, 33:2 (2010).
29 Unpublished study by Sasa Drakulic, cited in Rüdiger Wischenbart, 'Knowledge and its Price', *Publishing Research Quarterly*, 22:4 (2007), Winter.
30 Johan Heilbron, 'Structure and Dynamics of the World System of Translation', paper at the International Symposium on Translation and Cultural Mediation, UNESCO, 22–23 February 2010. Available at http://www.unesco.org/fileadmin/MULTIMEDIA/HQ/CLT/languages/pdf/Heilbron.pdf, accessed 26 February 2012.
31 ibid.
32 Gisèle Sapiro, 'Globalization and Cultural Diversity in the Book Market: The case of literary translations in the US and in France', *Poetics* 38 (2010), page 430.
33 Ibid., page 433.
34 Data on bestsellers was supplied to the author by Carlo Carrenho of PublishNews, which compiles regular charts available at http://www.publishnews.com.br/
35 Heilbron, op. cit.
36 See http://www.rochester.edu/College/translation/threepercent/
37 See http://www.rochester.edu/College/translation/threepercent/index.php?id=4712, accessed 28 September 2012.

The global book **115**

38 Lawrence Venuti, *The Translator's Invisibility: A history of translation*, 2nd edition, Routledge, 2008, page 5.
39 Interviewed by Nicholas Wroe, *Guardian*, 29 December 2012.
40 Interviewed by the author, 14 January 2013.
41 Dalkey Archive Press, *Research into Barriers to Translation and Best Practices: A study for the Global Translation Initiative*, March 2011. Available at http://www.dalkeyarchive.com/html/WYSIWYGfiles/file/Global%20Translation%20Initiative%20Study.pdf, accessed 20 December 2012.
42 Interviewed by the author, 23 January 2013.
43 Interviewed by the author, 5 March 2013.
44 Interviewed by the author, 20 December 2012.
45 Interviewed by the author, 20 December 2012.
46 Interviewed by the author, 23 January 2013.
47 Jaron Lanier, *Who Owns the Future?*, Penguin, 2013, loc 316 of 5429.
48 Francesco Pugliano, 'Microsoft, Google, and the future of Machine Translation', from blog *Localization in Silicon Valley*, 28 October 2011, http://rosecourt.wordpress.com/2011/10/28/microsoft-google-and-the-future-of-machine-translation/, accessed 5 October 2012.
49 The *AMO Times*, 28 January 2012. Available at http://www.theamotimes.com/2012/01/28/malaysian-eye-poked-over-google-translate-fail/, accessed 5 October 2012.
50 Nicholas Ostler, *The Last Lingua Franca: English until the return of Babel*, Penguin, 2010, pages 257–58.
51 David Bellos, *Is That a Fish in Your Ear? Translation and the meaning of everything*, Penguin, 2011, page 264 of 377 in ebook.
52 Huo Lee, in China Publishers Magazine, *Special Report for the London Book Fair 2012*, page 23. Available at http://publishingperspectives.com/2012/04/sponsored-post-report-from-china-publishers-magazine/?utm_source=feedburner&utm_medium=feed&utm_campaign=Feed%3A+PublishingPerspectives+%28Publishing+Perspectives%29, accessed 20 December 2012.

6

DIVERSITY AND CONVERGENCE

With the growth in the use of mobile devices, whether smartphones or tablets, consumers can access an array of content from just one device. The boundaries between different media can only blur further. What will be the difference between a book with multimedia content, a website, or a magazine? There is already little or no difference between a digital children's book with animations and different paths to follow, and a game. Experimentation, whether by authors, publishers, or other players, will offer great diversity to the user in the range of products and services which will become available, and the creators of content will have to think and collaborate in new ways.

Will books remain a differentiated product, or will we have new combined products such as the mook (magazine-book)? How will the connections develop between books, and to other content? Will content merge to enable users to create their own access points and curated or personalized selection? Will augmented reality on phones or glasses make available a wide range of content in new ways?

Semantic web

The notion of Web 3.0, the next generation of the internet, has some big implications for what the book will become. First, the development of the semantic web, as proposed by Tim Berners-Lee, would mean much more effective search as results are filtered by meaning and not just the relevance of the key words used. Search engines are already able to learn the behaviour of their users, and generate personalized results. For example, book lovers who search for Tolkien might see relevant results, more targeted towards the publications available, rather than, say, the Peter Jackson films. Google's Knowledge Graph was introduced in 2012 in a variety of languages and offers semantic search results which get closer to user needs – for example, it anticipates that if you search for the speech 'I have a dream' by Martin Luther King, you will want to find its text and a video clip. Advertisers are exploiting our search histories to target advertising in a highly effective manner – this is the power of so-called big data. This can go even further as our media and reading habits are analysed in even greater depth.

Once search engines, and other systems, have a more developed sense of the meaning of data, this will enable machines to talk to each other more effectively:

> The Semantic Web is not a separate Web but an extension of the current one, in which information is given well-defined meaning, better enabling computers and people to work in cooperation. ... these developments will usher in significant new functionality as machines become much better able to process and 'understand' the data that they merely display at present.[1]

For this to happen, the tagging of information has to be carried out more consistently so that semantics are encoded in sufficient depth that machines can work with it in a meaningful way.

The BBC has been working with the open content database MusicBrainz to make available relevant information about artists to music fans. Their service is using semantic tagging to pull in a range of information already available on the Web. The underlying principle is that there is little point in writing new material, but there is value to the user in collecting together a range of content. If you look up the entry for Lily Allen, it contains her Wikipedia biography and other links from the Web such as her own website, but also information on which tracks have been played on the BBC, when, and by which DJs. There are also links to BBC reviews of her albums, and relevant semantic connections such as that she is the daughter of the actor Keith Allen. He in turn is also a musician, appearing in the band Fat Les with Damien Hirst.

Matthew Shorter, Interactive Editor for Music, said in 2009:

> This is part of a general movement that's going on at the BBC to move away from pages that are built in a variety of legacy content production systems to actually publishing data that we can use in a more dynamic way across the web. ... The principle behind it is, let's try and drill down to the stuff that people are interested in. We're really interested in – instead of just physical releases – building in a concept of an album [or artist] as a kind of cultural entity.[2]

For content industries, the advantages of semantic tagging are that information can be found more readily by computer programs – this will aid discoverability. A step further is the possible creation of content by machines, drawn from relevant data sources. These sources would include government data, user-generated content, or published text, pictures, and video. Andrew Finlayson sees that as content is created in this fashion, there will be further challenges to our copyright and legal systems:

Data will be easily gathered and Web users will reuse the information and interpret it in their own ways. Such a world will challenge our notions of copyright law, fair use, and privacy as data start to flow without attribution or even verification. You can speculate that someday in the next 10 years machines combining parts of stories will commit libel by omitting critical context from data they have gathered and presented.[3]

As well as machines being able to create simple stories around sports events, the weather, and financial news, we can imagine the possibilities of users (and machines) gathering content for non-fiction books such as travel guides or local history titles. The commoditization of content in the areas of journalism and newspapers can only continue with machines developing this capability.

Whilst applications can already make use of content openly available on the web, much published content is not widely and freely available. Some publishers are starting to make datasets more easily available, and for example Pearson now makes some content open to app developers. In 2013 APIs (application programming interfaces) were offered both for Penguin Classics and for images for Dorling Kindersley. The API allows access to the content presented in a structured form. Upon registration, developers can make use of this content within their own apps, either with a suitable acknowledgement or (in the case of images) also upon the payment of a fee.[4] If a book is coded appropriately, and is made available as an API, anybody can then make a new interface or use for the content. This could be an interactive map of a travel book, an interface for *Pride and Prejudice* showing who is reading and their thoughts on each passage, or a biography linked to documentary material and relevant content from elsewhere on the internet. Such developments will enable book content to participate in the creation of the semantic web.

With augmented reality (AR), your view of the world is enhanced by computer technology. The development of such systems will enable users to access information which is highly targeted to their needs. For example, they may get location-based information on restaurants, shops, and sights as they walk around the centre of a city, with the screen of their mobile device showing them directions and content alongside the view of the places. This information could also be displayed on a headset or a pair of glasses, which are already in production by technology companies. The advent of such devices could also mean that rather than read a book on screen, you could simply have the text and images displayed on your glasses.

AR is already being applied to books, and in 2012 a picture book for the boy band One Direction was published (boxed with their album *Take Me Home*). If you downloaded the free app, you could then point your mobile device at the pages to access video content. This is an example of how a print object can work well with multimedia.

As search becomes ever more sophisticated, there is even the potential for the supremacy of text to be replaced. With some mobile phones you can already ask basic questions around simple searches, such as the weather in your area. This could become a much more developed conversation, where the verbal response is sufficient. There would be no need to sort through text results since the answer would be right for the context of your query to a high degree of accuracy. Adriaan van der Weel says:

> Textuality may appear to have been contingent on a series of historical circumstances that are now coming to an end. It may be on the verge of being replaced by different, more efficient forms of machine-to-machine and machine-to-human communications.[5]

What now for the book?

The realization of the semantic web is still some way off, and we cannot predict with any certainty how widespread its impact will be. In the mean time, text is still with us and the book is developing in interesting directions.

The possibilities of digital free the book from the constraints of the physical, in ways which are yet to be fully explored. The economics and the mechanics of adding in multimedia content can only become easier, and match the expectations of consumers of different kinds of media. With the possibility of updating a book in real time, the boundaries between a book and a website begin to become blurred. The writer and designer Craig Mod says that:

> The edges of digital books are becoming more porous – the technical distinction between a 'website' and a 'book' is now very thin. To move from 'website' to book is largely now a semantic distinction. Epub [an ebook format] is a bundle of HTML, zipped. As is mobi (Amazon's format). We zip up a collection of webpages and call it a 'book'. This is true not just for books but for all digital media. Digital allows us to take constituent parts of some media (individual music tracks, chapters in books) and, by drawing arbitrary lines around certain collections, define new 'albums' or 'books' in ways never possible in physical media.[6]

Tools will make it easier for users to curate their own collections and remix content, and share these with their friends, and this has implications for the licence under which they are accessing content. The actual experience of reading a book is already coming closer to reading web pages. With some ereading platforms, you can choose to scroll down the text rather than read using a page format. Live links can expand the functionality and the range of the book's content. Take the website of Pepys's diary, which publishes his original entries on a daily basis, and welcomes annotations from readers to add to thousands of pages of further information about the people and places which are mentioned. The overlays on maps highlight the relevant features of London in the seventeenth century.[7]

There are also disadvantages to a book becoming more like a website. There may be less emphasis on the quality of the design, such as the layout and

120 Diversity and convergence

typography. There is a relief to the author of a fixed and final point to a book, a finished version, which means that they are free from the curse of constant updating which attaches itself to a blog or a website. The relatively long lead time for the publication of books encourages a concentration on quality. The reader benefits from the author being given a deadline to finish their work, and being forced to come up with a considered and polished book. What is the version of record if the book is subject to constant change?

Digital frees the book from the constraints of print, and the length of the book can now expand – there is no restriction from the economics of printing or the weight of the printed book. A successful author writing for the mobile market in China may not want to bring their story to an end, if their readers are paying by the chapter. But such a text is distant from a well-rounded and finished work, and carries the risk of becoming rambling and lacking shape. It starts to resemble a serialized TV show which has reached its sell-by date. By contrast, in some Western markets, authors and publishers are experimenting with the publication of short stories and shorter books. Just as H. G. Wells saw the possibilities of a mass audience for books, writing *The Time Machine* as a novella in 1895, authors can see an audience for shorter works published in digital form.[8] This market largely went away when magazines stopped publishing short stories, and it is coming back through digital. Texts previously too short to make a whole book can be published in digital form, and the price adjusted to meet market expectations. Michael Bhaskar of Profile Books talks of their experimentation:

> We have done a few short-form titles, for example we have published something between a short story and a novella as an ebook only; we have published little collections of very short stories; we are also going towards the long-form journalism area. The good thing about all of this is that you just make it very cheap.[9]

Henry Farrell writes about the different dynamics of digital distribution:

> The length of the average book reflects the economics of the print trade and educated guesses as to what book-buyers will actually pay for, much more than it does the actual intellectual content of the book itself. … I suspect that people who would feel cheated if they paid 'book' price for a long essay (say around 20,000 words or so) will feel less so if they buy an electronic version. Ideally, we will end up in a world where people won't feel obliged to pad out what are really essays to book length in order to get published and compensated.[10]

For shorter non-fiction, there are other channels of communication available, however, and a regular blog post may find many more readers and a global audience.

The life cycle of the book has also changed away from the customary model of hardback → large-format paperback → mass market paperback. The book may start out as an ebook before moving into print. It may take the route of self-published → mainstream publication → backlisting as self-published ebook with the print edition available on demand. Its price as an ebook may fluctuate, from being given away free by the author, to being on special offer for one day only, or changing in quick order to discover its price elasticity (the degree to which demand reacts to changes in price). Authorship in turn takes on a hybrid character, moving between mainstream publication and indie publishing of ebooks and pbooks.

Is the book simply a container for content, or is it something greater than the sum of its parts? Many non-fiction titles can be broken down into individual chapters, which are then accessed separately. If it is information which the reader is after, this could produce a quick win. Just as traditional reference titles have migrated from whole book form to being accessed online through search or browsing functions, this path will lead to the erosion of the traditional form and boundaries of the book. Such a disaggregation of the book's form could lead to a generation unfamiliar with the shape and structure of a whole book. We have a whole food movement; now is the time to start a movement for whole books.

Adam Gopnik writes about the changes in how we listen to music, with the greater plurality of digital music and the loss of the old structures:

> My own teenage kids, as obsessed with music as I was, have an entirely different way of listening. They ignore the glowing-tube amp and classy articulate speakers in our living room; they bounce instead to tinny earbuds, and often spend hours listening to Taylor Swift or Radiohead on the still more tinny speakers of their computers. Sound quality seems secondary to some other thing they take from music. ... they a have a more limited conception of larger forms, of the record's two sides, of the symphony's three or four parts, of the swell and structure of a cantata. It isn't a question of classical tastes against pop; it's a question of small forms heard in motion against large forms heard with solemn intent. 'Sgt Pepper' baffles them as much as Beethoven's Ninth. They *snatch* at music as we snatched at movies, filling our heads with plural images.[11]

I wrote in chapter 2 about how with ebooks we lose some of the mental mapping present around the physical book. With a pbook we know where on the page something was, or how far back through the book. With an ebook there is a ready search function but we cannot simply flick back two-thirds of the way through a book, and find the passage we were looking for half way down the left-hand page.[12] This may not matter in the long run, but it perhaps explains why ebooks have made deeper inroads into genre fiction rather than non-fiction – in the UK the printed crime market fell by 25 per cent in 2012.[13] Craig Mod says that we have already lost our mental map of the book:

> Physicality is not an inherent part of digital no matter how hard you try (this is different than giving data edges, which is more about psychological

122 Diversity and convergence

relationships to collections of data than memory and physicality). But, we're gaining much more powerful tools – this is why super fast interfaces to all our highlights and notes we take in digital books is critical. We should be able to type just a few key words and have all the highlights related to those words appear with direct links into the books.[14]

What is striking about the development so far of the ebook is how it is the vanilla ebook – the plain text ebook – which has seen the fastest growth. Early predictions were that enhanced ebooks – with the addition of audio and video – would take off, and perhaps when reading *Pride and Prejudice* you would switch to a clip of the movie starring Keira Knightley as Elizabeth Bennet. With an AR function we could simply point our smart phone at the text of the novel. Similarly stories would be available with many different endings, at the press of your touch screen, offering the full realization of the visionaries of hypertext fiction.

In reality most readers would be irritated if their reading of a novel were interrupted by somebody else's depiction of the characters. They want to stimulate their own imagination, and they can watch the film version another time. Often if you really love a book, you don't necessarily want to see the film in any case. Mark Haddon says of his novel, *The Curious Incident of the Dog in the Night-Time*:

> It contains huge gaps that readers fill without noticing. … this, I suspect, is one of the reasons why so many of them feel a peculiar feeling of ownership about the book, for when they close the final page they have had an experience which is, to a large extent, of their own making.[15]

Further, if we want to enter a world of many different endings, and create our own characters, this can be satisfied through gaming. There is, however, renewed experimentation taking place around interactive fiction, where readers navigate through a complete story without the frustrations of never being able to complete all the levels of a game. Simon Meek of The Story Mechanics says that 'Games are naturally a collection of hurdles which you have to try and jump over to get to the end, and generally of increasing difficulty. That means that the majority of people don't finish the games that they start.' What is seen as a new opportunity in gaming is creating products with stronger stories. Users can be taken into an immersive environment – say London just before the Great War for the digital adaptation of *The Thirty-Nine Steps* – taking control of how much of this particular world they want to explore. Users can then manage the choices in the story without altering the basic story line. 'Everybody loves stories but not everybody loves consuming them in the format of the book', and this kind of product can appeal to a wider audience including 'lapsed gamers, those people who used to play games but don't any more – you could call them disenfranchised gamers, because the things which they once loved have now disappeared. That is definitely producing this notion of story and narrative in interactive experiences.'[16] Since everyone has access to interactive entertainment, through a whole range of devices, the market potential is significant.

Reading on digital devices may enable us to speed up our reading, but there is a danger that we simply revert to the power reading we employ on the web, where we are rushing to find the relevant fact or section. Books can facilitate relaxation, deep contemplation, and inspiration, and they are often to be savoured rather than rushed through – unless you are desperate to reach the denouement of a thriller. If the non-fiction book is disaggregated, this would render meaningless much narrative non-fiction and those books which develop a sustained argument. The convergence of media on to mobile devices is an opportunity for the book, but also a *risk*, since the distractions of other media are readily available. In a previous title, written with Bill Cope, we argued that a book is not a technology, it is an information architecture largely based around text.[17] This allowed for the fact that the book had already migrated from its physical form, and was not simply a product. But some are now arguing that the book is simply a container which can be broken up in the same way as the album was with the arrival of downloads. This argument is supported by a view of the book as the product of its technological and economic model in print. Authors and publishers acted in certain ways according to the boundaries set by print publication.

Clay Shirky argues that:

> maybe books won't survive the transition to digital devices, any more than scrolls survived the transition to movable type … the book is what you get when writers have access to printing presses, just as the album is what you get when musicians have access to LP-pressing machines. Take away the press, and what looked like an internal logic of thought may turn out to be a constraint of the medium.[18]

Those supporters of the book's continuing relevance, and this author is one of them, would dispute this observation. The form of the book does still work as a medium for narratives and sustained discussion or argument. Also, digital developments are seeing the book widen its boundaries to cover apps, enhanced ebooks, short-form writing, and interactive games. Books are becoming faster (quicker to market), authorship is becoming more democratic, with the growth in self-publishing, and readers can contribute to editorial decisions. The attraction for publishers to carry on using the terminology *book* is that it signifies quality and can, so far, command a higher value in the eyes of consumers. When Faber brought out their *Solar System* app in 2010, they still called it a book to separate it from other, lower-priced content. A book signifies something of value in education, for young children, or for posterity.

Free for all

The prospect is that business models from other parts of the media will shape the future of books. Cloud-based services mean that no longer need anybody actually

124 Diversity and convergence

own content. From a range of devices, users can and will be able to access films, music, TV, and books whenever they want. The library available will expand to the point where everything is there. In return for a simple monthly fee, subscription services negate the need to have physical copies of CDs, DVDs, or printed books. A higher fee offers more control over the content. The ultimate in decluttering, living spaces can achieve a minimalist look with cool and clean lines. In the short term there will be a bonanza for thrift or second-hand shops; whilst in many societies, living spaces are small flats or houses, and there is not the tradition of accumulating possessions over a life-time (or the household budget to enable such hoarding). You would not own your books but neither is this the case with the present models of how ebooks are licensed.

What are the downsides? Well, books do furnish a room, in Anthony Powell's phrase. For some generations there has been considerable attachment to printed copies of books, and part of the communications circuit through which a printed book moves involves its survival, often from one generation to another.[19] We may not mourn the replacement of cheaply bound paperbacks, but they still carry the memories of particular stages of our lives. Twenty-four-hour access to content relies on electricity and access to the internet, which can be unreliable even in the most developed societies. In societies controlled by totalitarian regimes, there is the risk of the cloud being turned off at times of civil unrest. Even if we are reading digitally, there will still be an attraction to having a quality printed copy to keep and display. This provides an incentive for books to be produced to a high standard of design and production, and for publishers to offer a bundle of ebook and pbook.

A factor driving the price of books down is the oversupply in the market. There are simply too many books available for anybody to read in a lifetime, there is no shortage of authors willing to write a book, there are many more forms of writing (from blogs to mobile fiction), and there are many more avenues through which a book can be published. The publisher's slush pile has moved online and a new author is expected to give their work away for free to attract an audience. Price is influential in online markets, and selling a book for as low as 20p appears to drive sales.

There are of course many free books already available, including editions of classic authors. There are already free downloads of the first few chapters of new titles, designed to entice you in, and this may become commonplace. Ads can be targeted around the paragraphs on which you linger, or which you highlight. A model of more ads and a lower price would also drive down the prices of ebooks. The author might allow it to be free, if they can watch your reading habits, with a view to improving their next book.

The anxiety is over the whole ecosystem of books if value disappears from the system in the way it has done from music and newspapers. There is less money available to pay authors, to pay for quality editing of text, and to produce high-quality type and illustrations. Some will say that quality will out, as readers migrate towards it, but there will be reduced incentives for authors to embark on long-term projects, and for publishers to invest in them. In the case of biography, academics can still plan for the long haul, but it is harder for a freelance writer, already hit by cutbacks due to recession:

> Advances have tumbled since 2008 so that the author who used to get £100,000 might now reasonably expect £15,000. And £15,000 doesn't go a long way towards supporting you for the five years that a large biography requires. For the self-employed, professional biographer it makes sense to go for a smaller project – something that can perhaps be written from printed sources.[20]

Physical bookselling is vital as a shop window for books, allowing browsing and for the covers of books to tempt those unfamiliar with the author's name. But its long-term future looks sure to follow that of high street record shops which could not adapt to the digital climate. Whilst online bookselling makes every title available, either in print or as an ebook, there is the need for the curation of titles to persuade readers to try something new, or else we face the prospect of a narrowing of what is read. There are already websites for the sharing of titles and opinions; programmes that will suggest titles based on your usage of social media; and ebook platforms which allow you to share your reading on Facebook and Twitter.[21]

Convergence

Convergence in the media is taking place on a number of fronts. The growth in the use of mobile devices is bringing the consumption of media on to one device, whether smartphone or tablet. In countries where the level of consumption of books is low, users are unlikely to be attracted to buying a separate ereader for books. For example in Brazil, the average number of books read per head is only two per year and this technology-loving nation is buying phones and tablets.[22] Phones are getting bigger – a phablet approaches the size of an ebook reader – whilst tablets are spawning a variety of portable formats. With a contract which gives you ready access to the internet, no one need be parted from social media, the latest news, their game of the moment, or even the latest bestselling book. Users then no longer care for the traditional media boundaries, or what kind of publisher has produced the app they are using or the video they are passing on to their friends. Newspapers offer a range of content from text to photo galleries, videos, and links to cats doing amazing things on YouTube. Content can be accessed through individual apps for books or magazines, or through social magazines such as Flipboard which combine the user's favourite content from social media and websites.

Convergence is not just a technological phenomenon, and users are joining up content from different media. There are curators working to do this on websites with particular flavours, and this is also being done by individual consumers of media. As Henry Jenkins says, 'convergence represents a cultural shift as consumers are encouraged to seek out new information and make connections among

126 Diversity and convergence

dispersed media content. ... Convergence occurs within the brains of individual consumers and through their social interactions with others.'[23]

Further convergence is taking place around tastes across the world, around brands and the latest media franchise. Since books are often where the franchises begin, whether Harry Potter, Twilight, or the Hunger Games, there is every opportunity for the book to remain a key part of the consumption. But the risk of venturing on to the device where other media is consumed, is that the reader is enticed off in other directions.

The next generation of readers

Ultimately the future of the book is driven by user behaviour amongst book consumers and readers. We can remain confident that there will be authors willing to write books, and across the world from the USA to India and China there is a strong desire amongst young people to write fiction for their generation. Authorship continues to grant status, and the book still has a powerful presence in a lot of societies, in the face of competition from a host of visual media. Books can be cool to new generations of readers, alongside movies and the latest fashion trend. With the decline in investment in journalism, there are fresh opportunities for the book to help explain what is happening in society. When the financial crisis hit the global economy in 2008, there was a surge of interest in books which tried to explain how the world had got itself into such a mess.

Text remains important. It seems likely that it developed as a model which works well with the wiring of our brains, and even simple words can have a powerful influence on our minds. Books are powerful tools, and they are an important repository of our society and culture. A significant element in the creation of the semantic web is trust – how can machines determine the most trustworthy and reliable sources of information? As we saw in an earlier chapter, one of the reasons why Google wanted book content in their databases was that they saw the value of this high-quality information. Considered, well structured and edited content will still be valuable in the future, and alongside this will continue the need for stories which develop our own imaginations.

Optimism has to be tempered by realism about the place of the book in the world. The evidence on IQ suggests that our vocabulary is more developed now, not as a result of leisure reading but from the complexity of the working world. Research on reading suggests that pupils do better at academic work if they also read for pleasure, but there are other forms of reading which have become important, mainly on the web. Reading of books has diminished faced with competition from other media, and the book has had to step aside, downgraded from prominence. The visitor to Paris in the 1920s, reading his Baedeker travel guide, would find that booksellers ranked second in importance in the section on shopping, after the department stores. This would not be the case in a modern travel guide, and the present-day traveller will most likely be consulting their smartphone for information. Taking the book on to mobile devices opens up the possibility of whole new readerships, but it also makes the book compete directly with the web, social media, games, videos, and a host of other content. We are used to quick wins in this environment, moving from one activity to another in quick succession, and long-form reading does not lend itself to the kind of multitasking which takes place, for example, when we watch television.

If we still believe, as this author does, that books should remain important in our society, then the most powerful driver is the impact of a generation of readers. The advocates of the book need to stand up and be counted, and ensure that it holds a prominent place in our world. Parents reading to their children, books being around in the home, investment in books in schools and libraries, reading groups, literacy programmes, city read initiatives – they all work towards creating the next generation of readers, and writers. There lies the future of the book.

Notes

1 Tim Berners-Lee, James Hendler, and Ora Lassila, 'The Semantic Web', *Scientific American* (2001), May.
2 Interviewed by Tim Ferguson in *BusinessWeek*, 21 January 2009. Available at http://www.businessweek.com/globalbiz/content/jan2009/gb20090121_970005.htm?chan=-top+news_top+news+index+-+temp_global+business, accessed 24 September 2013.
3 Andrew Finlayson, 'The Peril and Promise of the Semantic Web: What is the role of the journalist as computers become more adept at pulling together data from different sources?', *Nieman Reports* (2010), Summer, page 63.
4 For more information, see http://developer.pearson.com/
5 Adriaan van der Weel, *Changing our Textual Minds*, Manchester University Press, 2011, page 220.
6 Interviewed by the author, 1 February 2013.
7 See www.pepysdiary.com
8 Wells wrote the book first as five instalments for serialization in the *New Review* (from January to May 1895), and the book was published by William Heinemann in May. In an interview in the *New York Herald* in 1905 (15 April), Wells claimed to have written the story in a fortnight. See Bernard Bergonzi, 'The Publication of The Time Machine 1894–95', *The Review of English Studies*, New Series, 11:41 (1960), February, pages 42–51.
9 Interviewed by the author, 20 December 2012.
10 Henry Farrell, 'Towards a World of Smaller Books', blog at Crooked Timber. Available at http://crookedtimber.org/2010/02/09/towards-a-world-of-smaller-books/, accessed 29 December 2012.
11 Adam Gopnik, 'Music to Your Ears: The quest for 3-D recording and other mysteries of sound', *New Yorker*, 28 January 2013.
12 The X-Ray function in the Kindle platform offers a view of the structure of a book, such as its essential people or topics, but is still limited in its functionality.
13 *The Bookseller*, 1 February 2013, 'Review of the Year: Part four – genres'.
14 Interviewed by the author, 1 February 2013.
15 Mark Haddon, 'The Curious Incident's Origins', programme for the National Theatre stage production, June 2012.
16 Interviewed by the author, 19 March 2013.
17 Bill Cope and Angus Phillips (eds), *The Future of the Book in the Digital Age*, Chandos, 2006.
18 His comments featured in a response to a post on Nick Carr's blog entitled 'Will Gutenberg Laugh Last?', http://www.roughtype.com/?p=2296&cpage=1#comment-24085, accessed 19 February 2013.

19 Robert Darnton, 'What is the History of Books?', *Daedalus* (1982), Summer, pages 65–83. The model of the communications circuit was developed by Thomas R. Adams and Nicolas Barker in 'A New Model for the Study of the Book', in A. Barker, *Potencie of Life: Books in Society. The Clark Lectures 1986–1987*, British Library (1993), pages 5–43.
20 Kathryn Hughes, 'The Art of Biography is Alive and Well', *Guardian*, 15 February 2013.
21 For example, BookRx analyses your tweets and recommends books.
22 Average figure supplied by Carlo Carrenho, interviewed by the author, 19 March 2013.
23 Henry Jenkins, *Convergence Culture: Where old and new media collide*, New York University Press, 2006, loc 197 of 8270 in the ebook.

BIBLIOGRAPHY

Addey, Camilla, *Readers and Non-Readers: A cross-cultural study in Italy and the UK*, Legas Publishing, 2008.

Adermon, Adrian, and Liang, Che-Yuan, 'Piracy, Music and Movies: A natural experiment', IFN Working Paper, No. 854, 2010, Research Institute of Industrial Economics, Stockholm, Sweden.

Anderson, Chris, *Free: The Future of a Radical Price: The economics of abundance and why zero pricing is changing the face of business*, Random House, 2009.

Arnold, Martin, 'Making Books; placed products, and their cost', *New York Times*, 13 September 2001.

Association of Learned and Professional Society Publishers, *E-Book Strategies. The essential ALPSP guide on how to develop your e-book offer*, 2011.

Auletta, Ken, 'Citizens Jain: Why India's newspaper industry is thriving', *New Yorker*, 8 October 2012.

Babington Macaulay, Thomas, *Speeches on Copyright*, edited by Charles Gaston, Ginn, 1914.

Banou, Christina, and Phillips, Angus, 'The Greek Publishing Industry and Professional Development', *Publishing Research Quarterly*, 24 (2008).

Barker, Nicolas, *A Potencie of Life: Books in Society. The Clark Lectures 1986–1987*, British Library, 1993.

Baron, Dennis, *A Better Pencil: Readers, writers, and the digital revolution*, Oxford University Press, 2009.

Baverstock, Alison, *The Naked Author: A guide to self-publishing*, Bloomsbury, 2011.

Bellos, David, *Is That a Fish in Your Ear? Translation and the meaning of everything*, Penguin, 2011.

Bergonzi, Bernard, 'The Publication of The Time Machine 1894–95', *The Review of English Studies*, New Series, 11:41 (1960), February.

Berners-Lee, Tim, Hendler, James, and Lassila, Ora, 'The Semantic Web', *Scientific American* (2001), May.

Bhaskar, Michael, *The Content Machine: Towards a theory of publishing from the printing press to the digital network*, Anthem Press, 2013.

Bohn, Roger E., and Short, James E., *How Much Information? 2009 Report on American Consumers*, Global Information Industry Center, University of California, San Diego, December 2009.

Book Marketing Limited, *Expanding the Market*, 2005.

Bourdieu, Pierre, *The Field of Cultural Production: Essays on art and literature*, Columbia University Press, 1984.

130 Bibliography

——*Distinction*, translated by Richard Nice, Routledge, 2010.

Brand, Stewart (ed.), 'Keep Designing: How the information economy is being created and shaped by the hacker ethic', *Whole Earth Review* (1985), May.

Brienza, Casey, 'Books, Not Comics: Publishing fields, globalization, and Japanese manga in the United States', *Publishing Research Quarterly*, 25:2 (2009).

Brown, Jo, Broderick, Amanda J., and Lee, Nick, 'Word of Mouth Communication within Online Communities: Conceptualizing the online social network', *Journal Of Interactive Marketing*, 21:3 (2007), Summer.

Bustillo, Miguel, 'Library That Holds No Books', *Wall Street Journal*, 6 February 2013.

Campbell, Lisa, 'Fiction Rules 2012 E-book Sales', *The Bookseller*, 4 April 2013.

Carr, Nicholas, 'Is Google Making Us Stupid?', *The Atlantic*, July/August 2008.

Carrière, Jean-Claude, and Eco, Umberto, *This Is Not the End of the Book*, Harvill Secker, 2011.

Castro-Caldas, A., Petersson, K. M., Reis, A., Stone-Elander, S., and Ingvar, M., 'The Illiterate Brain: Learning to read and write during childhood influences the functional organization of the adult brain', *Brain*, 121 (1998).

Chalaby, Jean, 'The Making of an Entertainment Revolution: How the TV format trade became a global industry', *European Journal of Communication*, 26:4 (2011).

Chevalier, Judith A. and Mayzlin, Dina, 'The Effect of Word of Mouth on Sales: Online book reviews', *Journal of Marketing Research*, 43 (2006), August.

Christensen, Clayton M., *The Innovator's Dilemma: When new technologies cause great firms to fail*, Harvard Business School Press, 1997.

Clark, Christina, with Burke, David, *Boys' Reading Commission: A review of existing research to underpin the Commission*, National Literacy Trust, 2012.

Clark, Giles, and Phillips, Angus, *Inside Book Publishing*, 5th edition, Routledge, 2014.

Cloonan, William, and Postel, Jean-Philippe, 'Literary Agents and the Novel in 1996', *The French Review*, 70:6 (1997), May.

Coonan, Clifford, 'China's Mobile Phones Lead a Reading Revolution', *Irish Times*, 1 January 2011.

Cope, Bill, and Phillips, Angus (eds), *The Future of the Book in the Digital Age*, Chandos, 2006.

Cope, Wendy, 'You like my poems? So pay for them', *Guardian*, 8 December 2007.

Crystal, David, *English as a Global Language*, 2nd edition, Cambridge University Press, 2003.

Dalkey Archive Press, *Research into Barriers to Translation and Best Practices: A study for the Global Translation Initiative*, March 2011. Available at http://www.dalkeyarchive.com/wp-content/uploads/pdf/Global_Translation_Initiative_Study.pdf

Darnton, Robert, 'What is the History of Books?', *Daedalus* (1982), Summer.

Dehaene, Stanislas, *Reading in the Brain: The new science of how we read*, Penguin, 2009.

Dehaene, Stanislas, and Cohen, Laurent, 'The unique role of the visual word form area in reading', *Trends in Cognitive Sciences*, 15:6 (2011).

Denk, Jeremy, 'Flight of the Concord: The perils of the recording studio', *New Yorker*, 6 February 2012.

Desai, Anita, 'Author author: Aspiring writers from India', *Guardian*, 19 September 2009.

Egan, Jennifer, 'The Black Box', *New Yorker*, 4 June 2012.

Eliot, Simon, and Rose, Jonathan, *A Companion to the History of the Book*, Blackwell, 2007.

Entertainment Software Association, *Essential Facts about the Computer and Video Game Industry*, 2011.

Eurobarometer Survey, *European Cultural Values*, September 2007.

Eurostat Pocketbook, *Cultural Statistics*, 2007, 2011.

Fang, Cheng-Hsi, Lin, Tom M. Y., Liu, Fangyi, and Lin, Yu Hsiang, 'Product Type and Word of Mouth: A dyadic perspective', *Journal of Research in Interactive Marketing*, 5:2 (2011).

Featherstone, Mike, (ed.), *Global Culture: Nationalism, Globalization and Modernity*, Sage, 1990.

Finlayson, Andrew, 'The Peril and Promise of the Semantic Web: What is the role of the journalist as computers become more adept at pulling together data from different sources?', *Nieman Reports* (2010), Summer, page 63.

Flood, Alison, 'Romantic Fiction's Passion for Ebooks', *Guardian*, 10 October 2011.

Flynn, James R., *Are We Getting Smarter? Rising IQ in the twenty-first century*, Cambridge University Press, 2012.

Gandevia, Simon C., 'Savant-Like Skills Exposed in Normal People by Suppressing the Left Fronto-Temporal Lobe', *Journal of Integrative Neuroscience*, 2:2 (2003).

Gardiner, Juliet, '"What is an Author?" Contemporary publishing discourse and the author figure', *Publishing Research Quarterly* (2000), Spring.

Gillies, Mary Ann, *The Professional Literary Agent in Britain 1880–1920*, University of Toronto Press, 2007.

Goodyear, Dana, 'I Love Novels', *New Yorker*, 22 December 2008.

Gopnik, Adam, 'Music to Your Ears: The quest for 3-D recording and other mysteries of sound', *New Yorker*, 28 January 2013.

Grenier, S., Jones, S., Strucker, J., Murray, T. S., Gervais, G., and Brink, S., *Learning Literacy in Canada: Evidence from the International Survey of Reading Skills*, Statistics Canada, 2008.

Griswold, Wendy, *Regionalism and the Reading Class*, University of Chicago Press, 2008.

Gupta, Suman, 'Indian "Commercial" Fiction in English, the Publishing Industry, and Youth Culture', *Economic and Political Weekly*, 46:5 (2012).

Halinen, Irmeli, Sinko, Pirjo, and Laukkanen, Reijo, 'A Land of Readers', *Educational Leadership*, 63:2 (2005), October.

Hargreaves, Ian, *Digital Opportunity: A review of intellectual property and growth*, 2011. Available at http://www.ipo.gov.uk/ipreview

Healy, Michael, 'The Google Book Settlement: The end of the long and winding road?', *Logos*, 22:4 (2011).

Heilbron, Johan, 'Structure and Dynamics of the World System of Translation', paper presented at the International Symposium on Translation and Cultural Mediation, UNESCO, 22–3 February 2010. Available at http://www.unesco.org/fileadmin/MUL-TIMEDIA/HQ/CLT/languages/pdf/Heilbron.pdf

Hilligoss, Susan J., and Selfe, Cynthia L. (eds), *Literacy and Computers*, Modern Language Association (2004).

Horowitz, Anthony, 'The Battle for Books', *Guardian*, 28 February 2012.

Huang, Yun Kuei, and Yang, Wen I., 'Dissemination Motives and Effects of Internet Book Reviews', *The Electronic Library*, 28:6 (2010).

Hudson, Laura, 'Record-Breaking Kickstarter Turns Hamlet into a Choose-Your-Adventure Epic', *Wired*, 20 December 2012.

Hughes, Kathryn, 'The Art of Biography is Alive and Well', *Guardian*, 15 February 2013.

Hutton, Graeme and Fosdick, Maggie, 'The Globalization of Social Media: Consumer relationships with brands evolve in the digital space', *Journal of Advertising Research* (2011), December.

Isaacson, Walter, *Steve Jobs*, Hachette Digital, 2011.

Jaszi, Peter, 'Toward a Theory of Copyright: The Metamorphoses of "Authorship"', *Duke Law Journal*, 1:2 (1991), April.

Jenkins, Henry, *Textual Poachers: Television fans and participatory culture*, Routledge, 1992.

——*Convergence Culture: Where old and new media collide*, New York University Press, 2006.

Johns, Adrian, *Piracy: The intellectual property wars from Gutenberg to Gates*, University of Chicago Press, 2009.

Johnson, Catherine A., 'How do Public Libraries Create Social Capital? An analysis of interactions between library staff and patrons', *Library & Information Science Research*, 34 (2012).

Johnson, Steven, *Everything Bad is Good for You*, Allen Lane, 2005.

Jones, Graham, *Last Shop Standing: Whatever happened to record shops?*, Omnibus Press, 2010.

Kahneman, Daniel, *Thinking, Fast and Slow*, Penguin, 2011.

Kelly, Kevin, 'Scan This Book!', *New York Times*, 14 May 2006.

——'Reading in a Whole New Way', *Smithsonian* (2010), August.

Kilian, Thomas, Hennigs, Nadine, and Langner, Sascha, 'Do Millennials Read Books or Blogs? Introducing a media usage typology of the internet generation', *Journal of Consumer Marketing*, 29:2 (2012).

132 Bibliography

Kim-Renaud, Young-Key, Grinker, R. Richard, and Larsen, Kirk W., *Korean American Literature*, Sigur Center Asia Papers, 2004. Available at http://www.gwu.edu/~sigur/assets/docs/scap/SCAP20-KoreanWriters.pdf

Knulst, Wim, and Kraaykamp, Gerbert, 'Trends in Leisure Reading', *Poetics*, 26 (1998).

Knulst, Wim, and van den Broek, Andries, 'The Readership of Books in a Time of De-Reading', *Poetics*, 31 (2003).

Kotler, Philip, and Armstrong, Gary, *Principles of Marketing*, 9th edition, *Financial Times/Prentice Hall* (2001).

Kovač, Miha, *Never Mind the Web: Here comes the book*, Chandos, 2008.

Kovač, Miha, and Wischenbart, Rüdiger, 'A Myth Busted: Bestselling fiction in Europe and Slovenia', *Primerjalna književnost*, Ljubljana, 33:2 (2010).

Kretschmer, Martin, and Hardwick, Philip, *Authors' Earnings from Copyright and Non-copyright Sources: A survey of 25,000 British and German writers*, Centre for Intellectual Property Policy & Management, Bournemouth University, December 2007.

Kretzschmar, F., Pleimling, D., Hosemann, J., Füssel, S., Bornkessel-Schlesewsky, I., et al., 'Subjective Impressions Do Not Mirror Online Reading Effort: Concurrent EEG-eye-tracking evidence from the reading of books and digital media', *PLoS ONE*, 8:2 (2013).

LaChev, Anik, 'Fan Fiction: A genre and its (final?) frontiers', *Spectator*, 25:1 (2005), Spring.

Lamb, Christina, 'Is Obama Stalking You?', *Spectator*, 27 October 2012.

Lanier, Jaron, *Who Owns the Future?*, Penguin, 2013.

Larsen, Derek, and Watson, John J., 'A Guide Map to the Terrain of Gift Value', *Psychology and Marketing*, 18:8 (2001), August.

Lee, Hye-Kyung, 'Between Fan Culture and Copyright Infringement: Manga scanlation', *Media, Culture & Society*, 31:6 (2009).

Lenhart, Amanda, and Fox, Susannah, *Bloggers: A portrait of the internet's new storytellers*, Pew Internet & American Life Project, 19 July 2006.

Leontiadis, Ilias, Efstratiou, Christos, Picone, Marco, and Mascolo, Cecilia, 'Don't Kill My Ads! Balancing privacy in an ad-supported mobile application market', *HotMobile*, 12 (2012), 28–9 February.

Lessig, Lawrence, *Free Culture: How big media uses technology and the law to lock down culture and control creativity*, Penguin, 2004.

Locke, John, *How I Sold 1 Million eBooks in 5 Months*, Telemachus Press, 2011.

McCrum, Robert, 'So, what's this Globish Revolution?', *Observer*, 3 December 2006.

Macdonald, Liz, *A New Chapter: Public library services in the 21st century*, Carnegie Trust, May 2012.

McGuine, Hugh and O'Leary, Brian (eds), *Book: A Futurist's Manifesto*, O'Reilly, 2012.

McMillan, Graeme, 'Viewers are Flocking to Streaming Video Content – and so are Advertisers', *Wired*, 3 January 2013.

Mangen, Anne, 'Hypertext Fiction Reading: Haptics and immersion', *Journal of Research in Reading*, 31:4 (2008).

Markoff, John, 'The Passion of Steve Jobs', *New York Times*, 15 January 2008.

Martin, Jeff, and Magee, C. Max (eds), *The Late American Novel: Writers on the future of books*, Soft Skull Press, 2011.

Martin, Vanessa, Bunting, Catherine, and Oskala, Anni, *Arts Engagement in England 2008/09: Findings from the taking part survey*, Arts Council, February 2010.

Maslow, A. H., 'A Theory of Human Motivation', *Psychological Review*, 50 (1943).

Matthews, Nicole, and Moody, Nickianne, *Judging a Book by Its Cover: Fans, publishers, designers and the marketing of fiction*, Ashgate, 2007.

Menand, Louis, 'Show or Tell: Should creative writing be taught?', *New Yorker*, 8 June 2009.

Merkosi, Jason, *Burning the Page*, Sourcebooks, 2013.

Mesquita, Stephen, 'Trends in Travel Publishing in the US and UK Markets', *Logos*, 22:3 (2011).

Milgram, Stanley, 'The Small-World Problem', *Psychology Today*, 1:1 (1967), May.

Miller, Laura, 'Perpetual Turmoil: Book retailing in the 21st century United States', *Logos*, 22:3 (2011).

Milliot, Jim, 'Acting on Impulse', *Publishers Weekly*, 23 May 2011.

Morrissey, Brian, 'Marketer of the Year: Jeff Bezos', *Media Week*, 14 September 2009.

Mountford, Peter, 'Steal My Book! Why I'm abetting a rogue translation of my novel', *The Atlantic* (2012), November.

Mousse, Annina, 'The Characteristics of the Finnish Book Publishing Business', research paper, n.d. Available at http://www.uta.fi/FAST/FIN/RESEARCH/mousse.pdf

National Endowment for the Arts, *Reading at Risk: A survey of literary reading in America*, Research Division Report No. 46, June 2004.

——*Reading on the Rise: A new chapter in American literacy*, Office of Research and Analysis, January 2009.

Needleman, Sarah E., and Loten, Angus, 'When Freemium fails', *Wall Street Journal*, 22 August 2012.

Nielsen, *State of the Media: Consumer usage report*, 2011.

Nord, David Paul, Rubin, Joan Shelley, and Schudson, Michael (eds), *The Enduring Book: Print culture in postwar America*, University of North Carolina Press, 2009.

Noyesa, Jan M., and Garland, Kate J., 'Computer- vs. Paper-based Tasks: Are they equivalent?', *Ergonomics*, 51:9 (2008).

O'Connor, Anahad, and Hartocollis, Anemona, 'J. K. Rowling, in Court, Assails Potter Lexicon', *New York Times*, 14 April 2008.

OECD, *PISA 2009 at a Glance*, PISA, OECD Publishing, 2010.

——*PISA 2009 Results: What Students Know and Can Do – Student Performance in Reading, Mathematics and Science* (Volume I), PISA, OECD Publishing, 2010.

——*Let's Read Them a Story! The Parent Factor in Education*, PISA, OECD Publishing, 2012.

Ofcom, Communications Market Report: UK, Research Document, 4 August 2011.

Office for National Statistics, *General Lifestyle Survey Overview – a Report on the 2011 General Lifestyle Survey*, 7 March 2012.

O Instituto Paulo Montenegro e a ONG Ação Educativa, *INAF Brasil: O Indicador de Alfabetismo Funcional*, 2011.

Ostler, Nicholas, *The Last Lingua Franca: English until the return of Babel*, Penguin, 2010.

Pattuelli, M. Cristina, and Rabina, Debbie, 'Forms, Effects, Function: LIS students' attitudes towards portable e-book readers', *Aslib Proceedings*, 62:3 (2010).

Pew Research Centre, *The Rise of E-Reading*, report published 5 April 2012. Available at http://libraries.pewinternet.org/2012/04/04/the-rise-of-e-reading/

Pew Research Center, Global Attitudes Project, *Global Opinion of Obama Slips, International Policies Faulted*, 13 June 2012.

Pew Research Center, Project for Excellence in Journalism, *The State of the News Media 2012*, Major Trends, 2012. Available at http://stateofthemedia.org/2012/overview-4/major-trends

Pfanner, Eric, 'Copyright Cheats Face the Music in France', *New York Times*, 19 February 2012.

Phillips, Angus, 'Where is the Value in Publishing? The internet and the publishing value chain', *International Journal of the Book*, 2 (2005); reprinted in Alexis Weedon, *The History of the Book in the West: 1914–2000*, Ashgate, 2010.

——'Does the Book have a Future?', in Simon Eliot and Jonathan Rose, *A Companion to the History of the Book*, Blackwell, 2007.

——'The Digital Tide in Europe', paper given at the World Book Summit, Ljubljana, Slovenia, 31 March 2011.

Plester, Beverly, and Wood, Clare, 'Exploring Relationships Between Traditional and New Media Literacies: British preteen texters at school', *Journal of Computer-Mediated Communication*, 14 (2009).

Post, Chad W., *The Three Per Cent Problem: Rants and responses on publishing, translation, and the future of reading*, Open Letter, 2011.

Poupard, Duncan, 'Of Tombs, Traps and the Intrepid', *China Daily*, 3 August 2012.

Prahalad, C. K., and Ramaswamy, Venkatram, 'Co-Opting Customer Competence', *Harvard Business Review* (2000), January.

134 Bibliography

Putnam, Robert, 'Social capital: Measurement and consequences', *Canadian Journal of Policy Research*, 2 (2001).

PWC Report, *Understanding how US online shoppers are reshaping the retail experience*, 2012.

Rappaport, Edward, 'Copyright Term Extension: Estimating the economic values', Congressional Research Service, Library of Congress, 11 May 1998.

Rawlings, Ashley, and Mod, Craig, *Art Space Tokyo: An intimate guide to the Tokyo art world*, Pre-post, 2010.

Ren, Xiang, and Montgomery, Lucy, 'Chinese Online Literature: Creative consumers and evolving business models', *Arts Marketing*, 2:2 (2012).

Restak, Richard, *Mozart's Brain and the Fighter Pilot: Unleashing your brain's potential*, Three Rivers Press, 2001.

Robinson, John P., and Godbey, Geoffey, *Time for Life: The surprising ways Americans use their time*, Pennsylvania State University Press, 1999.

Rønning, Anne Holden (ed.), *Otherness: Essays and Studies 3.1*, Centre for Studies in Otherness, 2011. Available at http://www.otherness.dk/otherness-essays-studies-3.1/

Rowlands, Ian, Nicholas, David, Williams, Peter, Huntington, Paul, Fieldhouse, Maggie, Gunter, Barrie, Withey, Richard, Jamali, Hamid R., Dobrowolski, Tom, and Tenopir, Carol, 'The Google Generation: The information behaviour of the researcher of the future', *Aslib Proceedings*, 60:4 (2008).

Sapiro, Gisèle, 'Globalization and Cultural Diversity in the Book Market: The case of literary translations in the US and in France', *Poetics*, 38 (2010).

Schwartz, Barry, *The Paradox of Choice: Why more is less*, HarperCollins, 2004.

Scull, Christina, and Hammond, Wayne G., *The J. R. R. Tolkien Companion and Guide*, HarperCollins, 2006.

Shirky, Clay, *Here Comes Everybody*, Allen Lane, 2008.

Sieghart, William, *An Independent Review of E-Lending in Public Libraries in England*, report for the Department of Culture, Media and Sport, March 2013.

Snyder, Allan W., Mulcahy, Elaine, Taylor, Janet L., Mitchell, D. John, Sachdev, Perminder, and Sonjae, An, 'Literary Translation from Korean into English: A study in criteria', *Literature and Translation*, 11:1 (2002).

Southerton, Dale, Warde, Alan, Cheng, Shu-Li, and Olsen, Wendy, 'Trajectories of Time Spent Reading as a Primary Activity: A comparison of the Netherlands, Norway, France, UK and USA', Centre for Research on Socio-Cultural Change, Working Paper No. 39, November 2007.

Speer, Nicole K., Reynolds, Jeremy R., Swallow, Khena M., and Zacks, Jeffrey M., 'Reading Stories Activates Neural Representations of Visual and Motor Experiences', *Psychological Science*, 20:8 (2009).

Starkman, Dean, 'Major papers' longform meltdown', *Columbia Journalism Review*, 17 January 2013. Available at http://www.cjr.org/the_audit/major_papers_longform_meltdown.php?page=all

Steinle, Paul, and Brown, Sara, 'Embracing the Future', *American Journalism Review* (2012), Spring.

Stone, Brad, 'Amazon Erases Orwell Books From Kindle', *New York Times*, 18 July 2009.

——*The Everything Store: Jeff Bezos and the age of Amazon*, Little Brown, 2013.

Streitfeld, David, 'The Best Book Reviews Money Can Buy', *New York Times*, 25 August 2012.

——'App Writers Find Riches Are Elusive', *New York Times International Weekly*, 25 November 2012.

Sundara Rajan, Mira T., *Moral Rights: Principles, practice and new technology*, Oxford University Press, 2011.

Surowiecki, James, *The Wisdom of the Crowds: Why the many are smarter than the few*, Little, Brown, 2004.

Sveiby, Karl-Erik, 'A Knowledge-Based Theory of the Firm to Guide in Strategy Formulation', *Journal of Intellectual Capital*, 2:4 (2001).

Taleb, Nassim Nicholas, *The Black Swan: The impact of the highly improbable*, Penguin, 2007.

Bibliography **135**

Tapscott, Don, Ticoll, David, and Lowy, Alex, *Digital Capital: Harnessing the power of business webs*, Harvard Business School Press, 2000.

Thompson, John, *Merchants of Culture: The publishing business in the 21st century*, 2nd edition, Polity Press, 2012.

Tomlinson, John, *Cultural Imperialism: A critical introduction*, Continuum, 1991.

Toobin, Jeffrey, 'Google's Moon Shot: The quest for the universal library', *New Yorker*, 5 February 2007.

Turkle, Sherry, *Alone Together: Why we expect more from technology and less from each other*, Basic Books, 2011.

Twyla, Miranda, Williams-Rossi, Dara, Johnson, Kary A., and McKenzie, Nancy, 'Reluctant Readers in Middle School: Successful engagement with text using the e-reader', *International Journal of Applied Science and Technology*, 1:6 (2011), November.

van der Weel, Adriaan, *Changing our Textual Minds*, Manchester University Press, 2011.

Venuti, Lawrence, *The Translator's Invisibility: A history of translation*, 2nd edition, Routledge, 2008.

Waldfogel, Joel, 'Is the Sky Falling? The quality of new recorded music since Napster', column posted at Vox, 14 November 2011. Available at http://www.voxeu.org/article/was-napster-day-music-died

Waldman, Simon, 'The Best of British Blogging', *Guardian*, 18 December 2003.

Wang, Shaoguang, Davis, Deborah, and Bian, Yanjie, 'The Uneven Distribution of Cultural Capital: Book reading in urban China', *Modern China*, 32:3 (2006).

Westcott, Grace 'Friction over Fan Fiction: Is this burgeoning art form legal?', *Literary Review of Canada* (2008), July/August.

Wikström, Patrik, *The Music Industry: Music in the cloud*, Polity Press, 2009.

Wischenbart, Rüdiger, 'Knowledge and its Price', *Publishing Research Quarterly*, 22:4 (2007), Winter.

Wolf, Maryanne, *Proust and the Squid: The story and science of the reading brain*, Icon Books, 2008.

Yun, Qidong, 'State vs. Market: A perspective on China's publishing Industry', *Logos*, 24:1 (2013).

Zaid, Gabriel, *So Many Books: Reading and publishing in an age of abundance*, Sort of Books, 2004.

Zittrain, Jonathan, *The Future of the Internet: And how to stop it*, Yale University Press, 2008.

INDEX

Addey, C. 29
Adermon, A. 56
advertising 88–90, 117, 124
agents, literary 2
Amazon xiii, 4, 10, 19, 61, 66–67, 74, 80, 81, 88, 81–83, 113; reviews 80–81
Amis, M. 3
Anderson, C. 62
Apple 58, 66, 74, 76, 77, 78, 83
apps 88–89, 100, 118
Arnold, M. 90
augmented reality 118
Austen, J. 13, 40, 118, 122
Auster, P. 24
authorship 1–21, 103–5, 121; internet 9–11; self-publishing 4–7

Bacon, K. 65
Barnes 18
Bourdieu, P. 2, 19–20, 31
Bradbury, R. 41
Brand, S. 53–54
Brazil 32–33, 101, 106–7
Brienza, C. 105–6
Brin, S. 74
Bulgari 90
Burroughs, W. 61
business models 88–91

capital, forms of 91–92
capitalism 99–102
Carr, N. 44
Carrenho, C. 33, 101

Cesvet, B. 82–84
Chalaby, J. 101
Charney, D. 45
Che-Yuan, L. 56
China xii, 14–16, 26, 32, 45, 83, 87, 89, 100, 104, 109, 120
choice 78–79
Christensen, C. 75–76
Christie, A. 108
cinema *see* movies
class 31–33, 45
Clinton, H. 53
cloud computing 123–24
Coelho, P. 6–7, 64
collaboration 11–12, 67
consumer: experience 83–84; reviews 81, 92–93, 113
containerization xiv, 61, 121, 123
convergence xiv, 102, 125–26
conversational capital 82–84
Cope, B. 123
Cope, W. 63
copyright 51–55, 62–64, 66–70, 117–18
core-periphery model 109
Cox, J. 87
Creative Commons 53, 62
creative writing courses 3–4
Crystal, D. 102–3
cultural capital 31
culture 100–102; homogenization 106, 113
customer relationship 91–95

Index **137**

Danyté, M. 104
Davis, L. 5–6, 18, 35, 88
Del Rey, L. 57
democratization, of authorship 1–21
Denk, J. 58
Desai, A. 104
digital 100–101, 119–20; authorship 5, 12, 18; capital 88–95; copyright 53–63; globalization 112–13; publishing industry 75; reading habits 27, 35–38, 43–45, 123
digital rights management (DRM) 61, 63–66; social DRM 65
discoverability xiv, 77–80, 94
disintermediation xiii, 93–94

ebooks 42–43, 84–85, 121–22; advertising 89–90; authorship 5–6, 18; DRM 65–66; English language 110–13; lending 87–88, 91; market 73–77, 94–95, 101–2
Eco, U. 44, 107
Egan, J. 18
Ellory, R. J. 81
Emin, T. 68
English language 102–10; ebooks 110–13
ereaders 73, 76, 84, 125; reading habits 35–38, 42, 45
Etxebarria, L. 64
Europe 2–3, 28–30, 103

fair use 67, 69–70
fan fiction 9–10
Fangzhou, Y. 45, 104
Farrell, H. 120
Fifty Shades of Grey 11, 84, 103
Figes, O. 81
film *see* movies
Finland 30
Finlayson, A. 117–18
Flynn, J. 27–28
France 2, 26, 54, 56, 106
Frazier, C. 43
free content 52–54, 61–62
freemium 88–89
Friedman, J. 100

Gangnam Style 100
Gardiner, J. 7
gender 34–35, 42, 89
genre fiction 5, 8–11, 15, 42
Germany 3, 37, 56, 60
gifting 84–85
globalization xiv, 99–106, 109–13

Godbey, G. 25
Godin, S. 19
Godwin, D. 104
Goodkind, T. 64
Google 43, 44, 58, 69, 74, 111–12, 116–17
Gopnik, A. 121
Greece 30
Grisham, J. 8
Griswold, W. 32

Haddon, M. 122
Hargreaves, I. 61
Harry Potter 6, 10–11, 65
Heilbron, J. 108
Hemingway, E. 8
Higson, C. 7
Hocking, A. 6
Horowitz, A. 12–13
Howie, H. 5
Huang, J. 26, 35–36

illegal downloads *see* piracy
India 60, 104
Instagram 67
intellectual capital 91–92
intellectual property 69–70, 91–92
international literature 108–9
internet 73–75, 103, 116–17
Isaacson, W. 74, 102
Italy 29, 103

James, E. L. 11, 84, 103
Jenkins, H. 10, 125–26
Jobs, S. 74, 83, 102
Johns, A. 64
Johnson, S. 68
Jones, G. 77

Kahneman, D. 41
Kelly, K. 43, 54
Kindle 37, 74, 88
knowledge-based strategy 92
Korea 104–5, 110
Kovač, M. 103, 106, 110, 111

La Farge, P. 12
LaChev, A. 10
Lanier, J. 111
Larsson, S. 99, 104, 109
Lee, D. 105
lending 85–88
Lennon, J. 78
Lessig, L. 52–53

libraries 85–87
lingua franca 102–6
literary agents 2
Littell, J. 2
Locke, J. 4–5, 20, 81
Lord of the Rings 65
Luminous Airplanes 12

Macauley, T. 68
McEwan, I. 3, 46
MacLehose, C. 109
manga 68, 105–6
Mangan, A. 36–37
Mantel, H. 1
market 3, 106–7, 124; disruption 75–77;
  global 101–2; mobile 15
mash-ups 13–14
media meshing 34
Meek, S. 122
Menand, L. 3
Meno, J. 40–41
Meyer, S. 99
Mickey Mouse 69
Milgram, S. 65–66
Mills 95
mobile phone 100–101, 118–19; fiction on
  14–16, 32
Mod, C. 53, 119, 121–22
moral rights 54–55
movies 82–83
music industry 55–58, 61, 77–78

National Endowment of Arts 46
Netherlands 24–25, 26, 101, 103, 106
network model 93–95
newspapers 58–62, 100
North, R. 90–91
Norway 26, 103
Novikov, O. 63

Parks, T. 103
Patterson, J. 8
Pepys, S. 119
Phillips, N. 40
piracy 6–7, 55–56, 63–64
PISA 30, 45–46
plagiarism 13–14
Please Look after Mum 105
Popova, M. 20
Post, C. 108–9
Pottermore 6, 65
Powell, A. 124
Pride and Prejudice and Zombies 13
privacy 42, 84, 94–95

promotion, by authors 7–9
publication 120–21
publishers 1–2, 109–13; copyright 51–55,
  62–69; digital 73–84, 87–95
Putnam, R. 86

Qian Fucheng 15–16

Radiohead 57–58
Rajan, M. T. S. 54, 62
Ransome, A. ix
Rawlings, A. 53
reading 45–46, 122; class 31–33; decline
  of 24–28; digital 35–38; international
  28–31; other media 33–35, 126–27;
  science of 38–41; speed 37–38, 42–44
Restak, R. 43–44
reviews 81–82
Rice, C. 53
Robinson, J. P. 25
Rowling, J. K. xiii, 6, 10–11
Roy, A. 104
Rushdie, S. 8–9, 104
Russia xii, 7, 63

Sapiro, G. 106
scanlation 68
Schwartz, B. 79
science of reading 38–41
Self, W. 3–4
self-publishing 4–7
semantic web 116–19
sharing 56, 61
Shatzkin, M. 5, 45, 76–77, 79–80, 94–95
Shirky, C. 59, 123
short fiction 120
Shorter, M. 117
Simpson, J. 9
Six Degrees of Separation 65
Slovenia 103, 108, 110, 111
slow books 42–44, 45
smartphonc 34,
Smith, Z. 83
social capital 86–87
social media 8–9, 17, 66, 82–84, 125
sock puppets 81
Sony 73
Spain 60, 64
Spies, M. 79
Sputnik 25–26
Statute of Anne 51
Stezaker, J. 53
Stone, J. 56–57
Stop Online Piracy Act (SOPA) 64

stores 77–79, 125
Surowiecki, J. 90
Swallows and Amazons, ix
Sweden 56
symbolic capital 91, 95

Taleb, N. N. 102
Tartt, D. 8
technology companies 73–76, 88
teen fiction 28, 104
television 101–2
thinking 38–46
Thompson, J. 91
Tolkien, J. R. R. 10, 65, 67, 82
Tomlinson, J. 102
translation 106–13
Turkey xii, 101

United Kingdom 2–3
United States 25–26, 56, 69, 101
Updike, J. 7–8, 109

value 91–93
van der Weel, A. 119

Venuti, L. 109–10
verticals 95
video games 35–36, 122–23

Waldfogel, J. 57
watermarking 65
Watson, S. J. 21
Wattpad 9
Weisberg, J. 11
Weldon, F. 89–90
Wells, H. G. 120
whole books 121
Wikström, P. 57
Willis, B. 66
Wischenbart, R. 102, 106, 111
Wolf, M. 44
word of mouth 80–84
words, power of 41
world literature *see* international
    literature
Wright, M. 66

Zitwer, B. J. 105, 110
Žižek, S. 108